D0258952

advancing learning, changing lives

Edexcel GCSE
Physical Education

Student Book

Tony Scott

South Gloucestershire and Stroud College
Learning Resource Centre
WISE Campus
New Road
Stoke Gifford
Bristol
BS34 8LP
Tel: 0117 9192648

Acknowledgements

Pearson Education Limited
Edinburgh Gate
Harlow
Essex
CM 20 2JE
England

© Pearson Education 2009

The right of Tony Scott to be identified as the author of this work has been asserted by them in accordance with the Copyright, Designs and Patents Act 1988.

All rights reserved. No part of this publication may be reproduced, stored in a retrieval system, or transmitted in any form or by any means, electronic, mechanic, photocopying, recording or otherwise without either the prior written permission of the Publishers or a licence permitting restricted copying in the United Kingdom issued by the Copyright Licensing Agency Ltd, 90 Tottenham Court Road, London W1P 9EH

ISBN: 978-1-84690-372-4

Printed and bound in China (SWTC/07)
Edited by Helen Gough
Proof reading by Paul Edwards
Designed by Koichi Enomoto
Illustrations by Peter Bull Art Studio
Picture research by Sarah Purtill

The author would like to thank Yosef Smyth, Rebekah Taylor and Elaine Waterhouse for their help and support during the writing and production of this book. Also, Derek Rosenberg and the PE staff and students of the London Academy for their super efforts on the practical performance work on the ActiveTeach.
Also, my wife Louise for putting up with the hours I've spent over the computer keyboard while working on this project.

First edition 2009
10 9 8 7

The publisher would like to thank the following for their kind permission to reproduce their photographs:
(Key: b-bottom; c-centre; l-left; r-right; t-top)
Alamy Images: Aflo Foto Agency 27t; amana images inc. 46tc; Richard G. Bingham II 57tc; fStop 49b; Les Gibbon 12r; INTERFOTO Pressebildagentur 83bl, 96r; Jupiter Images / BananaStock 118; Roman Milert 117; William Nicklin 84; Photofusion Picture Library 15r; Photolibrary Wales 26b, 31; Alex Segre 121t; Tetra Images 150; Ian Thraves 100; Michael Weber 16cr; Janine Wiedel Photolibrary 15l; **Corbis:** Beathan 85l; Image Source 44; Andy Rain 10, 33t, 34l, 36; Reuters / Teddy Blackburn 40bl; Xinhua Press / Liang Qiang 21; zefa / Charles Gullung 136; **DK Images:** 48t, 49t, 89b, 130, 138l, 138c, 138r; Russell Sadur 80; **Getty Images:** 99; AFP / Adrian Dennis 60; AFP / Carl de Souza 106r; AFP / Fabrice Coffrini 110; AFP / Franck Fife 103; AFP / Francois-Xavier Marit 180bc; AFP / Jewel Samad 69r, 83c; AFP / Lluis Gene 178; AFP / Mark Ralston 153t, 153c; AFP / Paul Ellis 68; AFP / Ulrich Perrey 129; Alistair Berg 25; Michael Blann 94; Chris Cole 40tl, 172; Jeffrey Coolidge 89c; Julian Finney 33cl, 34c, 96c; Patrik Giardino 46t; John Gichigi 33br, 35cr, 53, 122; Alexander Hassenstein 180br; Mike Hewitt 58; Harry How 18, 153b; Isifa / Filip Singer 33tr, 34r, 175; John Giustina 39, 48b; Hannah Johnston 37; Ross Kinnaird 170, 174; Ross Land 111bl; Andy Lyons 41; NBAE / Otto Greule Jr 173; David Rogers 35br, 98, 111; Shaun Botterill 20, 70l, 152; Michael Steele 32; Stu Forster 38r, 120, 156; Ian Walton 33bc, 35cl; Howard Webb 108-109; **iStockphoto:** 88b, 88t; Christine Gonsalves 147; Steven Robertson 57c; Kelvin Wakefield 27c; **Jupiter Unlimited:** 33bl, 35l, 38l; AbleStock.com 55; BananaStock 54; Comstock Images 13b, 14t, 17, 45, 57t, 57b, 71; Goodshoot 141t; liquidlibrary 26t; Photos.com 16tl; Polka Dot Images 13c, 14c, 57bc, 59; Stockxpert 13t, 51, 52, 65, 69l, 121b, 124, 140t, 141b, 141c, 144, 188; Thinkstock Images 56, 70r; Jupiterimages: Imagezoo 67; Masakazu Watanabe 140b; **© 2008 The London Organising Committee of the Olympic Games and Paralympic Games Limited:** 24; PA Photos: AP / Andrew Medichini 106l; AP Photo / Al Goldis 160; EMPICS Sport / Mike Egerton 119; Tom Hevezi 14b; Chris Young 22; **Photolibrary.com:** Blend Images 85, 151; Digital Vision 76, 168; moodboard 114; **PunchStock:** Blend Images 137; Digital Vision 115; ImageState 16bl; RubberBall 50; **Rex Features:** Denkou Images 12l; Image Source 30; Timo Jaakonaho 40tr; Nils Jorgensen 40br; Martti Kainulainen 61, 83br, 89t, 96l; Lehtikuva Oy 128; Sipa Press 11, 23, 145

All other images © Pearson Education

Every effort has been made to trace the copyright holders and we apologise in advance for any unintentional omissions. We would be pleased to insert the appropriate acknowledgement in any subsequent edition of this publication.

Contents: delivering the Edexcel GCSE PE specification

Welcome to Edexcel GCSE PE

Is GCSE PE right for me?

The GCSE Physical Education course will appeal to you if you:

- have a keen interest in sport and recreation and always look forward to your PE lessons
- take part in sport/recreation outside of class time
- want to follow a course that develops knowledge and understanding through practical involvement
- want to know more about the benefits of sport and exercise
- want to improve your own performance in a range of sports roles
- want to study a course that is active and that you will enjoy
- are considering a sports-related career or an A Level/higher education course.

What will I be able to do taking this course?

It will give you exciting opportunities to be involved in a number of different physical activities, promoting an active and healthy lifestyle. You can perform in one or all of the following roles: player/participant, leader or official.

What will I learn?

You will:

- develop your knowledge and practical skills in a range of physical activities
- examine the effects of exercise and how training can improve performance
- find ways to improve your own performances in a variety of roles
- identify ways to develop and maintain a healthy and active lifestyle through participation in physical activity
- appreciate the benefits of promoting 'sport for all'.

How will I be assessed?

The GCSE course is assessed over two units:

Unit 1 is externally assessed through a written examination paper of 1 hour and 30 minutes. This will contribute a maximum of 40 per cent towards your total marks. The theory is broken down into two sections.

- The first, **healthy, active lifestyles,** requires you to develop an understanding of physical activity in relation to a healthy active lifestyle, looking at influences on involvement, fitness, training and diet.
- The second, **Your healthy, active body,** focuses on the body systems and structures and how they are developed through exercise.

Unit 2 is assessed in two sections:

- **Section 1** – four practical performances in the role of either player/participant, leader or official. You can achieve 48 per cent of the marks from your four performances, two of which may be in the role of a leader or official.
- **Section 2** – analysis of performance in one of the chosen activities. This will be worth 12 per cent of the marks and should include planning, performing and evaluating a Personal Exercise Programme.

What can I do after I've completed the course?

As well as being the ideal preparation for the A Level Physical Education course, GCSE PE allows for progression to related vocational qualifications, such as BTEC Firsts and Nationals in Sport or Sport and Exercise Sciences.

The course develops the transferable skills and key skills that employers are looking for and can lead to a wide variety of employment opportunities. This can include further training in such areas as recreational management, leisure activities, coaching, officiating, the fitness industry, the armed forces and the Civil Service.

How to use this book

Welcome to Edexcel GCSE PE! During this course you need to work hard to get the best mark possible – but you will also have fun doing it. This book will help you to do both!

If you take a look at the specification, you will see that this book is organised in exactly the same way, making it clear what you will cover and how.

Unit 1: The theory of physical education is divided into topics. Introducing each topic is a page which tells you what the topic is about and some questions to see how much you know before starting it. Each topic is then divided into chapters, breaking up the content into manageable chunks. You will find these features in each topic/chapter:

Objectives – each chapters starts with an objectives box so you know exactly what you are going to learn.

Edexcel key term boxes – there are certain terms that you will need to know, and also say what they mean. These boxes tell you exactly what they are.

Apply It activities – once you have learnt and understood something, the Apply It activities help you to apply your knowledge to really make use of it, as you will need to in both the exam and your practical assessment.

Edexcel examiner's tip – hints and tips to aid your learning and help you in the examination

Remember – learning the theory of PE isn't boring – it's what real sportspeople know in order to give their best performance. Also, theory material isn't only important for the written exam – it will help you perform your very best in the practical as well.

Uint 2: practical performance tells you about your practical performance, with tips from the examiner on how to achieve your best and what to look out for. It takes you through the practical performances, the Analysis of Performance and your Personal Exercise Programme, giving you everything you need in one accessible place.

We've broken down your revision into six stages to ensure that you are prepared every step of the way.

Zone in How to get into the perfect 'zone' for your revision

Planning zone Tips and advice on how to plan your revision effectively

Know zone All the facts you need to know and exam-style practice at the end of every topic and section (in the theory). Here are some other useful features at the end of topics:

You should know: a check-yourself list of the concepts and facts that you should know before you sit the exam.

Edexcel Key terms: make sure you can understand and apply important terminology.

Stretch and support activities: tasks to help you apply the material in each topic and link it to your own interests or personal exercise programme.

Practice Exam Questions: concluding each topic are some real past paper questions to test your understanding.

Don't panic zone Last-minute revision tips for just before the exam

Exam zone Help on how to answer different question types

Zone out What do you do after your exam? This section contains information on how to get your results and answers to frequently asked questions on what to do next.

ResultsPlus

These features are based on the actual marks that students have achieved in past exams. They are combined with expert advice and guidance from examiners to show you how to achieve better results.

There are four different types of ResultsPlus features throughout this book:

ResultsPlus
Exam Question Report

Jared is part of the school athletics team and has been described as a "natural athlete". His running style is excellent and other performers comment on how he looks when he runs. What is the term used to describe the appreciation of the beauty of a skilful performance?
(1 mark, June 2008)

Answer

The correct answer is: Aesthetic appreciation

How students answered

Some students got this wrong (38%). This is not a difficult question but you have to know the exact term to get this right. Some students answered:

Student answered – sportsmanship = wrong!!!

Student answered – sport appreciation = wrong!!!

| | 38% | 0 marks |

Most students got this right (62%). It is essential to get these types of questions correct if you are going to get a good mark in the examination.

| | 62% | 1 marks |

Exam question reports show previous exam questions with details about how well students answered them.

• Red shows the number of students who scored low marks

• Green shows the number of students who did well.

They explain how students could have achieved the top marks so that you can make sure that you answer these questions correctly in future.

ResultsPlus
Watch out!

The **reasons** why people take part in physical activity are sometimes referred to as **benefits**. This can be confusing.

Watch out! The examiner knows where students tend to do things well and also where they can go wrong. So pay attention to these – they could really help you save or gain marks!

ResultsPlus
Build Better Answers

Which of the following statements describes a physical benefit of exercise? (1 mark)

A   Meeting new people

B   Gaining an aesthetic appreciation of movement

C   Feeling better about body shape

D   Improving body shape

Correct answer: D

Examiner: Students who answered C could have mixed up feeling better about their body shape, which is mental, as opposed to improved body shape, which is physical.

These features give you a question, the correct answer and some concise useful information about the content area or question type.

Maximise your marks are featured in the Know zone at the end of each topic. They include an exam-style question with a student answer, examiner comments and an improved answer so that you can see how to build a better response.

Unit 1: The Theory of Physical Education

The theory is tested in a single examination that is worth 40 per cent of your final grade. It is broken down into two sections covering everything from personal influences to the effect of diet on bones. Short course students will only study section 1 of the theory for their examination.

Section 1: Healthy, active lifestyles

Why do people get involved in physical activity? What are the benefits of taking part in sport and exercise on well-being? This section will help you understand the answers to these two important questions which in turn will help you understand your own and others' motivations. Also, you will learn how important such factors as exercise, training, fitness and diet are to success and the benefits they bring in everyday life.

Topic 1.1: Healthy, active lifestyles and how they could benefit you

Many people enjoy healthy, active lifestyles; gaining many physical, mental and social benefits.

Topic 1.2: Influences on your healthy, active lifestyle

This topic covers the influences on people getting involved in sport and looks at what is done to keep them coming back and reaching the top.

Topic 1.3: Exercise and fitness as part of your healthy, active lifestyle

This topic deals with the relationship between health, exercise and fitness. It also looks at the specific areas of fitness required to lead a healthy, active lifestyle and to improve performance.

Topic 1.4: Physical activity as part of your healthy, active lifestyle

The building blocks to create a programme to get fit are the principles of training. You also need to know which methods of training to use to achieve your goals and finally how to assess whether your training is having the desired effects.

Topic 1.5: Your personal health and wellbeing

It's not only about fitness and skills; there are other things that go into building a healthy, active lifestyle and athlete such as balancing diet, work and rest.

Unit 1

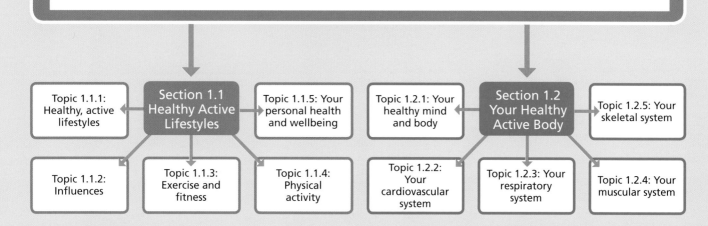

Theory 40%
Written examination 80 marks (40 short course)

Topic 1.1.1: Healthy, active lifestyles

Section 1.1 Healthy Active Lifestyles

Topic 1.1.5: Your personal health and wellbeing

Topic 1.2.1: Your healthy mind and body

Section 1.2 Your Healthy Active Body

Topic 1.2.5: Your skeletal system

Topic 1.1.2: Influences

Topic 1.1.3: Exercise and fitness

Topic 1.1.4: Physical activity

Topic 1.2.2: Your cardiovascular system

Topic 1.2.3: Your respiratory system

Topic 1.2.4: Your muscular system

Section 2: Your healthy, active body
This section looks at your body, starting with the different body types. You will then look at the body systems, such as the cardiovascular and respiratory systems. The body systems work differently during exercise and can be enhanced from regular exercise. They all work together to help you cope when taking part. Lifestyle choices also affect them in different ways, resulting in benefits or potentially leading to problems.

Topic 2.1: Physical activity and your healthy mind and body
The link between body composition and sport is looked at in this topic. In addition, optimum weight, problems with weight, safety, and drugs in sport are just a few of the other areas covered.

Topic 2.2: A healthy, active lifestyle and your cardiovascular system
In this topic you will learn how your lifestyle affects your cardiovascular system, what happens when you are exercising, and the effects of exercising regularly.

Topic 2.3: A healthy, active lifestyle and your respiratory system
You breathe faster during exercise and after certain activities you are left gasping for breath well after it has finished, in this topic you will find out why. You will also see how your lifestyle can affect your respiratory system.

Topic 2.4: A healthy, active lifestyle and your muscular system
In this topic you will learn about specific muscles, what occurs when you are actually exercising, and the effects of exercising over a long period of time. You will also learn what happens when you build up muscles (hypertrophy) and what will happen if you stop training or are injured (muscle atrophy).

Topic 2.5: A healthy, active lifestyle and your skeletal system
Your skeleton supports and protects you. It is also designed specifically to allow movement, meaning you can kick a football or do somersaults.

Topic 1.1.1: Healthy, active lifestyles and how they could benefit you

Sport in Context

Yoga is enjoyable, can present challenges and satisfies many of the requirements of an active healthy lifestyle while building confidence and self-esteem. It offers much more than the opportunity to stretch and breathe.

Yoga brings physical, mental and social benefits. It makes the body more flexible and builds strength. It can help you to cope with the pressures of life, and participants benefit from the good feeling that results from 'taking part': all mental benefits. Attending yoga classes will add to your social life; you'll meet new people and make new friends!

In Topic 1.1.1 you will learn that a healthy active lifestyle is made up of three things: social, mental and physical wellbeing. Yoga is one of a variety of physical activities which leads to all these benefits.

PE and me

Think about your own involvement in physical activity:

1. What sports or activities do you take part in?

2. Which is your best activity?

3. What benefits do you gain from taking part in this activity?

4. Are these benefits social, mental or physical?

Compare your answers with the rest of the class.

Topic Overview

By the end of this topic you should be able to:

● classify the reasons or benefits of taking part in physical activity and sport;

● explain how people benefit from taking part in sport;

● explain what participation in physical activity can stimulate.

1: The three categories of a healthy, active lifestyle

Objectives

At the end of this chapter you should be able to:

- explain what constitutes a healthy, active lifestyle
- classify the benefits of a healthy, active lifestyle as physical, social or mental.

edexcel ⠿ key terms

Healthy, active lifestyle: a lifestyle that contributes positively to physical, mental, and social wellbeing, and includes regular exercise and physical activity.

edexcel ⠿ examiner tip

Mental benefits are often referred to as psychological benefits. Either of these terms can be used.

A healthy, active lifestyle has a positive effect on physical and mental wellbeing. People who exercise regularly and have an active social life with a network of friends tend to cope better with the stresses of daily life.

There are many and varied opportunities for anyone who is interested to take part in all kinds of physical activity. Most participants are amateurs who pay to take part; although in school most sport is free. Some professionals are paid to take part, to coach or to teach others. These are the lucky few who are paid to do what they enjoy.

Reasons for and benefits of taking part in physical activity

Benefits fall into three main categories:

- physical (improving health and fitness)
- mental/psychological (reducing stress and relieving related problems)
- social (making and developing friendships and building teamwork skills)

The table lists the various benefits in more detail.

Physical	Social	Mental (Psychological)
Contribute to good physical health	Mix with others	Relieve and/or prevent stress and tension
Physical challenge (Can I do it?)	Make new friends	Mental challenge (Can I do it?)
Increase fitness	Meet current friends	Increase self-esteem and confidence
Improve performance	Develop teamwork/ cooperation	Help the individual feel good
Improve any of the health-related exercise factors: cardiovascular fitness muscular strength muscular endurance flexibility body composition	Work with others	Contribute to enjoyment of life
		Aesthetic appreciation

2: Benefits of taking part in physical activity

Objectives

At the end of this chapter you should be able to explain how a healthy, active lifestyle can:

- increase individual wellbeing
- help the individual to feel good (serotonin)
- help relieve stress, and prevent stress-related illness
- increase self-esteem and confidence
- contribute to good health
- contribute to enjoyment of life.

We have already looked at how to classify the benefits of taking part in physical activity into physical, social, or mental categories. This section looks at why physical activity brings about these benefits.

LINK IT UP!

Later in the course, when planning your personal exercise programme (PEP), you will see how a programme of planned, well-thought-out exercise can improve fitness. See topic 2.2.5.

Turn to p.99 to find out more about how diet relates to a controlled weight loss programme.

Exercise and physical activity help to improve cardiovascular fitness, increase strength, improve body composition and flexibility, and tone muscles, all of which can:

- increase fitness
- help the individual feel good
- help relieve stress, and prevent stress-related illness
- increase self-esteem and confidence
- contribute to good health
- contribute to enjoyment of life
- provide a mental challenge

These are the main reasons why people take part in physical activity. As each is described, you may want to refer to the table on p.11 to remind yourself of whether it is classified as physical, social, or mental.

1. To increase fitness

Exercise, training, and taking part in physical exercise can increase fitness. A programme of planned, well thought-out exercises, resistance training and playing sport is a good way to achieve this. Muscles can be strengthened and made more flexible, becoming more toned in the process.

Exercising and playing expends energy, which uses up calories. This can contribute to a controlled weight loss programme, although this is best achieved alongside a controlled diet.

2. To help the individual feel good

Many people take part in physical activity, play sport, or embark on an exercise programme because they want to feel good. Exercise can literally make you feel good. It produces serotonin – the 'feel-good' hormone – so it is not just good for the heart, lungs, muscles and bones, but also for the mind. Regular physical activity improves fitness and body shape, and helps participants to look and feel better. It follows that exercise can help people with low self-esteem.

3. To relieve stress and tension

Physical activities can provide a distraction from the problems of daily life, and can relieve stress and tension caused by work, school, and family pressures. Although exercise cannot solve problems, it can make them easier to face by providing a complete distraction for a while.

4. To increase self-esteem and confidence

Many activities provide a physical challenge. Overcoming such a challenge gives a sense of achievement which can lead to an increase in self-esteem and confidence.

For example, it is very difficult to complete the London Marathon. People who do manage to complete it improve their self-esteem. They are likely to have more confidence when taking on other tasks that seem difficult.

Apply it!

Here are some quotes of people who have run the London Marathon:

'I was struggling badly after 18 miles but the cheers of the crowd, constantly shouting my name got me through. An amazing day!'

'I finished 15 minutes behind what I did the last time 20 years ago and am delighted that careful training compensated somewhat for the passing years!'

'Running the London marathon is an experience to say the least! There are not many races that you can run alongside Mr Blobby, sausages and rhinos!!'

'When finished, you feel like you did something that at first was too big, too hard, too much for you to take on. Yet you did… You realise that not only have you got the ability to surprise others but you also have the ability to surprise yourself.'

Talk about the benefit of taking part in the London Marathon each person gained.

5. To improve health

People who are physically fitter usually cope better if they become ill. This applies not only in the case of common colds or flu, but also, many scientists believe, in the case of serious illness.

The ability to withstand and recover from illness is related to fitness, and we will see how heart and lung function improves with exercise. So exercise and sport contribute to good health.

6. For enjoyment

Most people who practise some form of physical activity do so because they enjoy it. Observe the players at the local sports centre or tennis courts – they are probably there because they want to be.

Enjoyment of physical activity may be affected by the reason for participating in it. Some people are forced to do it. Others are highly competitive and want to win. Some take part because they know it's good for them.

7. For a mental challenge

Many sporting activities provide a mental as well as a physical challenge. The London Marathon is a tough physical challenge, but it is an equally tough mental challenge – the thought of running 26 miles and 365 yards (42.195 kilometres) can be very daunting, especially for someone who has never run that distance before.

Apply it!

For each of the reasons (1–7) in this section, think of one example of a physical activity which you could use to illustrate or explain the point. You could collect photos or cuttings. The photograph shows one example – practising yoga can help to relieve stress.

ResultsPlus
Build Better Answers

Which of the following statements describes a physical benefit of exercise? (1 mark)

A Meeting new people

B Gaining an aesthetic appreciation of movement

C Feeling better about body shape

D Improving body shape

Correct answer: D

Examiner: Students who answered C could have mixed up feeling better about their body shape, which is mental, as opposed to improved body shape, which is physical.

3: Reasons for taking part in physical activity

Objectives

In exam questions based on this topic, you will be expected to be able to explain how participation in physical activity can stimulate:

- cooperation
- competition
- physical challenge
- aesthetic appreciation
- the development of friendships and social mixing.

We have already thought about why taking part in physical activity leads to certain benefits. This section looks at more of these benefits (or reasons for participation), many of which are related to working in teams, with a partner, or in groups. These benefits (or reasons for participation) include:

1. cooperation
2. competition
3. physical challenge
4. aesthetic appreciation
5. the development of friendships and social mixing.

Most activities offer an opportunity to benefit from one or more of these.

1. Cooperation

Many sports are played in teams. Working in groups helps to improve **teamwork and cooperation**, which are often necessary in everyday life. Netball, football, rugby, and hockey are all good examples of team sports where it is important to support and encourage your team-mates.

2. Competition

Competition can be thought of as psychological (mental) both in terms of the psychological preparation necessary to compete and in terms of getting away from the stresses of life. When competing most people put aside their problems and concentrate on doing well in their sport.

3. For a physical challenge

Coming back to sport after a long time away, perhaps as an adult who has not taken part since leaving school, or taking on a seemingly impossible task, allows for a physical challenge which can be very satisfying. The London Marathon is a good example because the challenge it offers is often the most striking memory for those who take part for fun.

4. Aesthetic appreciation

Moments in sport are sometimes beautiful, although this aspect of sport may not always be appreciated as much as winning. Beauty may be seen in a brilliantly executed goal or a save in football, a try in rugby, a jump shot in basketball, a passing shot in tennis, a smash in badminton or table tennis, a cover drive in cricket or a delicate chip in golf. Often it is the observer who appreciates the performer, although hitting a cover drive in cricket can feel brilliant; sometimes the performer knows when something just feels right. Sports such as ice dancing or gymnastics, tend to be more often thought of in these terms.

5. Development of friendships and social mixing

Taking part in exercise or sport at school or at a club means involvement with other people, including fellow participants, coaches and trainers, and officials. Participants get to know more people, make new friends and develop lasting friendships.

Training alone can be quite lonely and requires motivation and discipline, but most activities present opportunities to mix socially. Many clubs have a strong social side. They are frequently run by volunteers, and extra volunteers are usually welcomed.

Apply it!

Try to think of one person (or a group of people) you know whom you met through sport. Write down which sport it was, and how you met, and compare what you have written with the rest of your class.

Apply it!

Here are two other quotes from participants in the London Marathon.

'I finished behind Gordon Ramsay but ahead of Ben Fogle. I was really disappointed in my time, a long way off what I'd been aiming for.'

'One of my training partners finished a minute in front and the other just behind. We started out together but got split up after five miles and never saw each other till we crossed the finishing line.'

Discuss the reasons these runners might have had for taking part.

ResultsPlus
Exam Question Report

Jared is part of the school athletics team and has been described as a "natural athlete". His running style is excellent and other performers comment on how he looks when he runs. What is the term used to describe the appreciation of the beauty of a skilful performance?
(1 mark, June 2008)

Answer

The correct answer is: Aesthetic appreciation.

How students answered

Some students got this wrong (38%). This is not a difficult question but you have to know the exact term to get this right. Some students answered:

sportsmanship = wrong!!!

sport appreciation = wrong!!!

	38% 0 marks

Most students got this right (62%). It is essential to get these types of questions correct if you are going to get a good mark in the examination.

	62% 1 mark

examzone

Know Zone
Topic 1.1.1: Healthy, active lifestyles and how they could benefit you

In this topic your will learn about the reasons why people choose to take part in a healthy, active lifestyle and the wide variety of benefits they can get from this, not just the physical but also the social and mental benefits.

You should know...

- ☐ What constitutes a healthy active lifestyle
- ☐ How to classify the benefits of a healthy active lifestyle as physical, social or mental
- ☐ How a healthy lifestyle can:
  - increase individual wellbeing
  - help the individual to feel good
  - help relieve stress and prevent stress-related illness
  - increase self-esteem and confidence
  - contribute to good health
  - contribute to enjoyment of life.
- ☐ How participation in physical activity can stimulate:
  - cooperation
  - competition
  - physical challenge
  - aesthetic appreciation
  - the development of friendships and social mixing.

Key terms

Healthy, active lifestyle
Self-esteem

Stretch activity

Think about this topic when you are playing or watching sport and see if you can apply your knowledge and explain how the terms are being applied. For example, aesthetic appreciation of a great shot in tennis that just hits inside the baseline and is impossible to return, or in football if the goalkeeper makes an impossible save from a great shot at goal.

Support activity

You can almost certainly use this knowledge when you are planning your personal exercise programme (PEP) by giving your reasons for including certain activities and explaining the benefits you will gain from including them in your programme.

Examiner's tip

Look out for questions on this topic in the examination as you may be required to give reasons why someone would take part or to list the benefits of taking part. Remember why you chose certain activities for your PEP and the benefits you gained from performing them. Remember aesthetic appreciation – visualise a great moment in sport such as Tom Daley diving into the pool to help you explain.

ResultsPlus
Maximise your marks

Question: Complete the statements below about the benefits gained from participating in practical activity.

▲ (i) Many people take part in physical activity to _____stress. This is a_____benefit of physical activity. (2)

Students' answer	Examiners' comments	Build Better Answers
i) lose	This is correct. Other common correct answers were lower, reduce, relieve and psychological. Most students (over 70%) gained very good marks on this question.	

▲ (ii) Weight loss as a result of physical activity is a physical benefit of exercise. Weight loss could also have a mental benefit to the individual, for example, _____(1)

ii) make them feel better	This is correct. An easy explain question – these are the easy parts so you must get these correct.	

☐ (iii) Weight loss as a result of physical activity is achieved by _____ (1)

iii) doing exercise and building up muscles	This answer would not get you a mark on this question, because you must get over the point that you need to use more calories than you take in – energy balance.	Using more calories in your daily exercise than your daily intake in your diet

☐ (iv) Some people take part in physical activity for the _____ benefits, for example, it allows them to meet new people and make new friends. (1)

iv) Social	The student has given a correct answer – one of the three reasons you must know and easy to recall.	

◯ (v) People who take part in physical activity, especially activities such as gymnastics and dance, can gain an _____ appreciation of the activity due to the quality of the movements being performed. (1)

v) Mental	This is incorrect. Be careful – 2 out of every 3 candidates dropped a mark on this question.	The correct answer was aesthetic.

Few candidates got full marks for this question and some of the parts are one word answers which are either correct or wrong so you must know them. Try to remember the three reasons for taking part plus aesthetic appreciation = the beauty of the performance.

Practice Exam Questions

1 Which of the following statements describes a physical benefit of exercise?

A   Meeting new people

B   Gaining an aesthetic appreciation of movement

C   Feeling better about body shape

D   Improving body shape

2 Year 11 students were asked why they took GCSE PE. Some answers are listed below.

a) Categorise each of their answers, stating whether the answers are a mental, physical or social benefit of exercise.

I took it because lots of my friends took it

I hoped it would help me to lose weight

I enjoy physical education lessons

Topic 1.1.2: Influences on your healthy, active lifestyle

Sport in Context

Many things can influence people to become involved in sport, such as friends, family or simply enjoying it on TV. Cristiano Ronaldo had a family connection with football; his father was the kit man for the first amateur team he played for, Andorinha. You will learn about several of these influences in this topic, including family, role models, image, and other aspects such as age, disability, gender and race.

People cannot easily continue to be involved unless they have access to the right resources. Would you want to travel 5 hours to train every weekend? The importance of cost, location, and availability of resources is discussed in this topic. You will also learn about government initiatives which can help you reach your goals as a performer, official, leader or volunteer.

PE and me

1. What do you think influenced you to become involved in sport?

2. How important were those influences?

3. How would you feel if it cost £10 to get into your local sports hall?

4. Can you think of anything that promotes participation in sport?

Topic Overview

After this topic you will be able to:

- explain and understand the influences on people to participate in physical education
- explain a number of initiatives to get and keep people involved in physical education
- explain the sports participation pyramid.

4: Influences on taking part

Objectives

When you have completed this chapter, you will be able to identify the main factors that affect involvement in physical activity. These include:

- people: family, peers, role models
- image: fashion, media coverage
- cultural factors: age, disability, gender, race
- resources: availability, location, access, time
- health and wellbeing: illness and health problems
- socio-economic: cost, status.

Many factors affect participation in physical activity. Personal circumstances may influence both choice of activity and the extent to which someone takes part. People who enjoy participating while young are more likely to continue to take part as they get older, although their role may change from participant to coach, official, or volunteer.

1. People

Most people's choice of activity is, to a greater or lesser extent, influenced by others. People tend to choose the same activities as their friends, or members of their family.

Family Children frequently take part in the same physical activities as their parents. They also often follow the same sports and support the same teams.

Peers The influence of the peer group – people of the same age – is very important. It is much easier to succeed in any activity with the encouragement and support of friends.

Role models These are people whose actions are emulated by others. They can be a variety of people in different roles. Successful sportsmen and women, such as Rebecca Adlington, David Beckham, Kelly Holmes and Chris Hoy, are often in the media spotlight and may become role models, inspiring others to take up the same sport. For example, fans of Andy Murray may feel inspired to join their local tennis club. Being a role model brings with it responsibilities – for example, not to take drugs and get into fights.

Apply it!

Ask the other members of your group what their mother's or father's favourite sport is, and which team(s) they support. Then ask the other group members the same questions. Record your answers.

2. Image

Fashion Many activities require the 'right' equipment – e.g. you need boots to play football. Some brands of sports equipment can be very fashionable – and expensive – partly as a result of media coverage of famous sportspeople. Sales of sports equipment and clothing are influenced by the time of year. For instance, sales of tennis equipment increase around Wimbledon fortnight, and more fitness clothing and equipment are sold around New Year.

Media coverage The media influences many people's choice of physical activity. Media coverage increases the popularity of some sports. The London Marathon is an excellent example: many competitors are inspired to take part by watching the race on TV. In this case, the media has a strong and positive effect.

Apply it!

Think of someone who has inspired you. Get some photographs of your role model and use them to put together a short presentation explaining why they are good at what they do, and what makes them a great role model.

3. Cultural factors

Disability People with disabilities can take part in many activities. Resources and opportunities for disabled people to take part in sport are increasing – as the success of the British team at the Beijing Paralympics shows – but more availability is still needed at a local level for people with disabilities who are not international athletes.

Age Age can affect performance and may also influence participation in physical activities. In most sports it is good to start young, although some competitive events may have age restrictions. For example, the minimum age for taking part in the London Marathon is 18. Work and family responsibilities, as well as health problems, may prevent adults and older people from participating in physical activities.

Gender The idea that some physical activities are more or less exclusively male and others female has more or less disappeared, but some activities still offer one sex more opportunities than the other. A boy who loves netball may struggle to find a team, while (arguably) women's cricket and football are taken less seriously than men's.

The public perception of an activity can also be a problem. Perhaps girls hesitate to play football because it is mainly depicted as a men's sport by the media.

Race Taking up a sport or activity may be influenced by ethnic background. For example, there are proportionally fewer black tennis players or golfers than there are footballers.

There have been instances of racist abuse against coloured players, most notably in soccer. In 2008, Paul Ince became the first black person to become a manager in the Premiership.

edexcel ::: **examiner tip**

Questions on this section are likely to be open questions which require a longer answer. You may be asked to evaluate all these influences, so you should know them all as your answer will be worth several marks.

4. Resources

Availability If people are to take part in physical activity and sport, suitable facilities and resources must be available.

Location Participation in sport depends on what is locally available. Some places may not have any facilities for some activities.

Access Facilities need to be easily accessible. If they cannot be reached by foot or bike, easy access by public transport (bus or train) is important. Good parking may also be a consideration.

Time Facilities need to be available at the right time. This probably means that they should be open in the evening and at weekends, and, for students, during school holidays. Participants need to make time for practising and training.

The England Women's Cricket Team retained The Ashes in Australia in 2008

Apply it!

In your group, compare the coverage of men's and women's sport, for example in football, rugby, golf, tennis, cricket, and the Olympic Games. Take some newspapers and look at the sports pages. How many stories are about women's sport, and how many about men's?

5. Health and wellbeing

Illness Individuals who are ill cannot take part.
Health Problems These can affect participation in physical activities. For example, people who have asthma may not be able to take part in activities which involve a lot of running, although swimming might be good for them. However, many people go to the gym or play a sport they enjoy as a way of staying healthy.

6. Socio-economic

Cost Most activities have some associated costs – hire of facilities, lessons, equipment, shoes etc. If people cannot afford to take part, their socio-economic status has influenced their involvement.
Status This relates to a person's current situation or position in society e.g. employed, in education or looking for work. Status can affect participation in physical activity as people may not have time. Alternatively, status can influence the type of sport a person is involved in, or enjoys to watch.

Some sports, such as running, are quite inexpensive. Football may require boots and club membership, but these costs are minimal compared with, for example, golf, which requires a lot of expensive equipment and annual club fees.

LINK IT UP!

Go to www.runsweet.com and investigate diabetes and sport. You could also visit www.transplantsport.org.uk.

LINK IT UP!

Go to Paralympics London 2012 www.london2012.com and/or Paralympics Beijing www.paralympics.org.uk if you want to investigate this topic further.

5: Opportunities for getting involved in sport

Objectives

At the end of this chapter you should be able to:

- Explain opportunities to become involved in physical activity, including leadership, officiating and volunteering

- Describe a number of initiatives developed to encourage participation in physical activity, including:
  - minimum involvement in PE
  - PE School Sport and Club Links (PESSCL)
  - School Sport Partnerships
  - Sport England's Start, Stay, Succeed initiative
  - the Youth Sport Trust's TOP and Active Kids Programme.

Most activities offer opportunities to participate in a variety of roles, including teaching or coaching, officiating, and volunteering. Training opportunities are available through most sports' governing bodies. For example, the Badminton Association of England has a coaching programme endorsed by the United Kingdom Coaching Certificate (UKCC), which offers training in a variety of roles to encourage young people to stay involved. Participants can start with their 1st4Sport Level 1 Certificate in Coaching Badminton and progress through the levels. The programme is designed to encourage long-term involvement in sport: participants may begin as performers and continue to be involved as coaches or officials.

Many sports depend on volunteers. Even the London 2012 Olympic Games and Paralympic Games will rely on voluntary effort.

ResultsPlus
Build Better Answers

Which of the following is a correct statement in relation to Sport England's 'Start, Stay, Succeed' objectives?

A   Start – plan so that every child starts the school day with physical activity to increase participation and improve health.

B   Start – increase the number of adults who start their day with exercise.

C   Stay – aim to keep officials working in sport so that development costs are reduced.

D   Succeed – create opportunities for talented performers to achieve success.

Correct answer: D

Examiner: If you read the options carefully you may be able to eliminate B because it refers to adults only.

The London 2012 Olympic Games and Paralympic Games will create opportunities for many people to get involved in sport in completely different roles: athletes will take part; officials will be needed to ensure the rules are not broken and the events are safe; and volunteers will be required to prepare and help the day-to-day running of the games.

Initiatives to keep people involved

It is important to know about the latest policies on PE and school sport. Initiatives change over time so check their official websites for the most up-to-date information.

1. Government Initiatives

Recently the government introduced a policy to 'ensure all pupils receive their entitlement to two hours of high quality Physical Education (PE) per week'. This will encourage more participation and improve students' fitness.

2. PE School Sport and Club Links (PESSCL)

The government set up the PE School Sport and Club Links (PESSCL) strategy to increase the take up of sporting opportunities by 5–16 year olds.

- Sport England and the Youth Sport Trust manage two important areas in the Club Links and Step into Sport programmes. These provide opportunities for young people to take part in sport as performers, leaders, officials and also as volunteers through the Step into Sport programme.

- The PESSCL programme aims to strengthen links between schools and local sports clubs.

3. School Sport Partnerships

School sport partnerships are based around a group of schools with a sports college at the center, or hub. The aim of the scheme is to develop sporting opportunities in a wide range of sports and offer high quality coaching and competitions within the local community.

4. The organisation Sport England

This organisation believes sport has the power to change people's lives. Sport England is committed to creating opportunities for people to *start*, *stay* and *succeed* in sport.

Start: increase participation in sport in order to improve the health of the nation, with a focus on priority groups.

Stay: retain people in sport through an effective network of clubs, sports facilities, coaches, volunteers and competitive opportunities.

Succeed: create opportunities for talented performers to achieve success.

5. The Youth Sport Trust TOP Link

TOP programmes are designed to encourage people of all abilities to get involved in sport. TOP link is aimed at encouraging students in the 14–16 age group to organise and manage sports activities and dance festivals in local primary and special schools. Students who are taking Physical Education GCSE or who have taken awards in, for example, sports leadership are offered the opportunity to put their skills to good use. Their experience as a leader or official may even count towards their GCSE.

6. Active Kids programme

Various supermarkets and other enterprises run voucher programmes in which vouchers collected by parents can be used by schools to buy sporting and other equipment. One example of these is the Active Kids programme.

6: Sports participation pyramid

Objectives

At the end of this chapter you should be able to explain the sports participation pyramid in regard to the foundation, participation, performance and elite stages.

The Sports participation pyramid illustrates the development from mass participation at the base of the pyramid to excellence at the top. The greater the number of people who become involved in sport through participating and volunteering, the broader the base. The broader the base, the more likely it is that some will achieve excellence.

Participation: this is the stage when young people begin to participate regularly in a specific activity for enjoyment.

○ Sports development contributes significantly to this stage with its community TOP programme (after school coaching), school festivals, multi-skills clubs and club/school links.

○ Sports clubs become important at this stage as they make the link to the next stage of development.

Foundation: this is the base of the pyramid. At this stage most participants are likely to be learning/experiencing basic sporting skills. The types of activity which contribute to this stage include:

◉ primary PE lessons

◉ Top Play activities (sports development)

◉ multi-sports sessions (sports centres).

The acquisition of good exercise/skill habits provides a basis for personal development and future participation in a chosen sport.

Ex

Perf

Part

Fou

Elite/Excellence: this stage is the peak of the pyramid, where individuals reach sporting excellence.

- The pyramid narrows here as fewer people take part at this level.

- Governing bodies of sport are responsible for development at this level as players pass from county to regional to national squads.

Performance: during this stage young people begin to concentrate on sport specific skills and to develop talent in specific sports.

- Quality coaching is an essential part of player development at this level. The following schemes contribute to this:

  - Organised by sports development-coaching weeks: Shropshire youth games.

  - Other: Active sports, club activity.

Apply it!

Draw a pyramid and see if you can label each stage according to the sports participation pyramid. Once you've done this try explaining each stage.

Where do you think you are on the pyramid?

examzone

Know Zone
Topic 1.1.2: Influences on your healthy, active lifestyle

Some of the points in this topic may have had an influence on you taking part in sport and even in the actual sports you play. The terms influences, involvement and opportunities are the key words in this topic.

You should know...

☐ Identify the key influences and opportunities that affect involvement in physical activity. These include:
- people: family, peers, role models
- image: fashion, media coverage
- cultural factors: disability, age, gender, race, religion
- resources: availability, location, access, time
- health and wellbeing: illness and health problems
- socio-economic: cost, status.

☐ Explain opportunities to become involved in physical activity, including:
- minimum involvement in PE
- PE school sport and club links (PESSCL)
- school sport partnerships
- Sport England's Start, Stay, Succeed initiative and the Youth Sport Trust's TOP and Active Kids Programme.

☐ Be able to explain the sports participation pyramid with regard to the foundation, participation, performance and elite stages.

Key terms

Influences
Involvement
Opportunities
PESSCL

Sports participation pyramid
Start, stay, succeed
School Sport partnerships
Youth Sport Trust

Stretch activity

In the introduction to your PEP explain your involvement in your sport. How were you introduced to it? How are you affected by access, availability, opening times, travel, cost, etc? What are the opportunities in your sport? You could use the sports participation pyramid: applying it will help you to remember it.

Support activity

Think about your influences. For example, if you play football for a club outside school, why did you first start? Did a friend (peer), mother (family), one of your neighbours (people) or your 'big brother' (family or could be your role model) take you there first?

Examiner's tip

Make sure you remember IIO:

I = influences   **I** = involvement   **O** = opportunities

If you are involved how have any of these factors affected you? If you are not involved in sport in that position, are there any sports stars or role models who have made the top in their sport and can you apply this to them?

Question: Tom and Jack are taking GCSE Physical Education because they enjoy all the activities. Since they were very young they have been influenced in the sports they like by others. Give three ways that they could be influenced by people into taking part in sport. (3 marks)

Students' answer	Examiners' comments	Build Better Answers
Family = their father or mother takes part in the sport e.g. father plays rugby or mother is a good swimmer.	⚠ This is correct. The student identified that family may have influenced them and gave an example.	
Brother = they started because their brother played.	⬤ This is wrong. The student has already identified that family (brother) can be an influence, losing them a mark.	Explaining that a friend might have influenced them would have given them a mark. A friend might have encouraged them to join a local team.
Role model = they are influenced by a star performer and want to copy that person.	⚠ This is correct. Some role models stand out over a long period of time even when their careers are over. David Beckham would be an example of this.	A role model could also be a family member, or even a teacher!

Remember under the 'people' heading comes family, friends and role models. Use these headings to think of how they can influence the boys.

If you remember the people heading and the three influences included in it, you should be able to build your answer around each one. Also think of how you and or your friends became involved in sport.

Remember the other influence headings, such as **Image**: fashion, media coverage – as the influence question may be on that heading.

Practice Exam Questions

1 Place the number for each heading against the correct row of key influences that can impact on taking part in physical activity. 1 Cultural; 2 Health and wellbeing; 3 People; 4 Image (4)

   A   family, peers, role models_____   B   illness and health problems_____

   C   fashion, media coverage_____   D   age, disability, gender, race_____

2 Explain what is meant by the 'sports participation pyramid'. (1)

3 Which of the following is referring to the sports participation pyramid? (1)

   Foundation, participation, performance, elite   PE school sport and club links

   School sport partnerships   Start, stay, succeed

Topic 1.1.3: Exercise and fitness as part of your healthy, active lifestyle

Weight Training

Weight training is one method of training that is used by many professional athletes and also by many people who simply wish to improve their general fitness and health. Weight training is particularly beneficial because it builds muscle giving you greater strength. Theo Walcott started weight training when he joined Arsenal at the age of 16, as part of his training programme. This has had a big impact on his performance, and has helped make him an important player for Arsenal and England.

However, weight training is no good in isolation. In order to get the best results, it must be combined with an overall training programme which takes into account your aims, and then looks at your other physical needs such as cardiovascular fitness and a good diet.

PE and me

1. How do you think fitness affects performance?

2. Think about the types of training you have taken part in, what do you think they improve?

3. How do you think improvements from training improve performance?

4. How many skills can you list?

Topic overview

After you have finished this topic you should know about:

◉ health, exercise, fitness and performance, and how they relate

◉ the five aspects of health-related exercise

◉ the six components of skill-related fitness.

7: Health, exercise, fitness and performance

Objectives

Understand the terms:

⊙ health

⊙ exercise

⊙ fitness

and understand how they relate to performance in physical activities and a healthy lifestyle.

Exercise improves **health** and develops **fitness**, which enhances **performance** in physical activities. In the next pages you will learn how:

⊙ health

⊙ exercise

⊙ fitness

⊙ performance

relate to each other and how they are defined.

edexcel key terms

Health: a state of complete mental, physical, and social wellbeing and not merely the absence of disease and infirmity.

Health

Health is not merely the absence of disease and infirmity. It is a positive state of complete mental, physical, and social wellbeing. Health can be improved by taking part in exercise as it builds up fitness levels. This should allow people to lead an active life and get through their daily life more comfortably. Regular exercise also helps to keep people healthy by preventing illness.

edexcel key terms

Exercise: a form of physical activity which maintains or improves health and/or physical fitness.

Exercise

Although infectious diseases have become less widespread in the western world over the past 100 years, health problems caused by lack of exercise have increased. Such conditions are called hypokinetic diseases, and include heart disease, high blood pressure and back pain. Hypokinetic diseases can be relieved by taking exercise. Exercise is also thought to relieve stress and tension; one way is that it can distract people from their everyday lives. Taking part in exercise also increases fitness levels which has a number of different benefits.

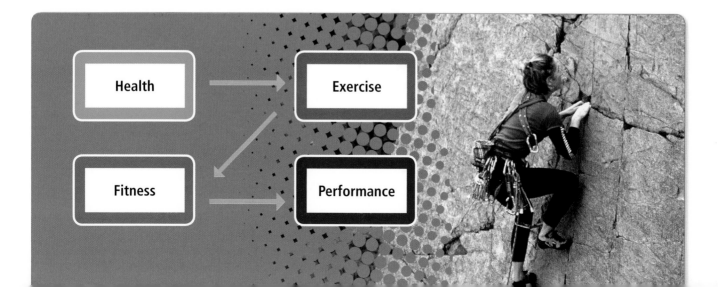

---

edexcel ⠿ key terms

Fitness: ability to meet the demands of the environment.

Fitness

To most people, being fit means being able to cope with the demands of everyday activities, such as school, college, work and home. People also exercise to improve their fitness, so that they can lead an active life without undue strain on their health and, in some cases, so that they can participate in sports and physical activities at a higher level. Awareness of the need to exercise and keep fit has grown over the last few years; the benefits of a healthy, active lifestyle are listed in Topic 1.1.1 (p. 11). Fitness also contributes to enhanced performance.

For example, players who are fit can run further and faster, hold off more tackles, hit more good shots and get into better gymnastics positions.

Results Plus

Build Better Answers

Explain the term performance

Correct answer: How well a task is completed

This is the easiest of the four definitions, and you must get this right in the exam.

---

edexcel ⠿ key terms

Performance: how well a task is completed.

Performance

Performance is taking part in an activity to the best of one's ability, whether it's Sunday afternoon football in the park or playing in the Premiership, playing tennis at the local club or competing at Wimbledon. Players at every level must exercise to keep themselves fit and enhance their performance.

Fit but not healthy

It is possible to be fit but not healthy. Many sportsmen and women suffer debilitating injuries and illnesses.

- Dame Kelly Holmes, 800m and 1500m Olympic gold medallist, missed the Atlanta Olympics in 1996 as a result of injury and the Sydney Olympics in 2000 because of illness. However, she won two gold medals at the Athens Olympics in 2004 where commentator Steve Cram exclaimed, 'What a race. What a performance.'

- Sir Steven Redgrave, an Olympic gold medallist for rowing, has diabetes and ulcerative colitis (a severe bowel condition), but these conditions have not stopped him from winning five Olympic gold medals.

8: The five components of health-related exercise

Objectives

Know and understand the components of health-related exercise:

- cardiovascular fitness
- muscular strength
- muscular endurance
- flexibility
- body composition

and understand how they relate to different physical activities.

You have learned about the three main reasons for taking part in physical activity and the four definitions of health, exercise, fitness and performance. To improve fitness and performance, you will learn that the five components of health-related exercise need to be developed: cardiovascular fitness, muscular strength, muscular endurance, flexibility and body composition.

These five elements help us to stay physically fit and healthy. You must know and understand these terms, and be able to explain, apply and describe them.

Cardiovascular fitness

Health

Exercise

Muscular strength

Muscular endurance

Health-Related Exercise

Fitness

Performance

Flexibility

Body composition

Cardiovascular fitness describes the efficiency of the heart, lungs, and blood vessels to deliver oxygen to working muscle tissues so that prolonged physical work can be maintained. A strong heart and clear blood vessels are necessary to supply the muscles with plenty of oxygen via the blood. Cardiovascular fitness is the most important aspect of health-related exercise, as it is closely concerned with the fitness of the heart and the lungs. It enables people to follow a healthy, active lifestyle without undue fatigue, and to continue to take part in sport and be physically active throughout the whole of life. It can be improved by training.

This is the fitness that is required to allow sportsmen and women to play long hard matches in football, rugby, netball, tennis and many other sports. A high level of cardiovascular fitness is essential for all athletes, from skiers to badminton players, from footballers to dancers. It is crucial to developing other types of fitness.

Muscular strength enables the lifting of very heavy weights, e.g. weightlifting. It is important if work or a particular sport involves the exertion of great force. Muscular strength can be developed by lifting heavy weights with few repetitions or by high-intensity strength work.

It is particularly important in such activities as weightlifting where the competitor is required to make one massive effort, but is also required in games such as rugby where the two packs push against each other in a scrum trying to drive the opponents backwards. It is often associated with steroids as they can help develop muscular strength and help the athlete recover quickly and so train harder (although the use of steroids is dangerous to health and illegal in competition).

Muscular endurance enables muscles to be exercised repeatedly without getting unduly tired, for example in activities such as running and swimming.
It is necessary for many sports and physical activities. Some form of training to improve this area of fitness, such as press-ups or sit-ups, is included in most exercise programmes.

Muscular endurance is often associated with games such as tennis which take a long time and require strong shots at the end of the game as well as at the beginning. It is an important part of general fitness, since many people need muscular endurance in their everyday life. Doing the daily chores or working in the garden are obvious examples.

edexcel ::: **key terms**
Muscular endurance: the ability to use the voluntary muscles many times without getting tired.

LINK IT UP!
The five components of health-related exercise are all **physical** benefits of exercise.

edexcel ::: **key terms**
Muscular strength: the amount of force a muscle can exert against a resistance.

LINK IT UP!
Both muscular strength and muscular endurance are covered in more depth in Topic 1.1.4.

edexcel ::: **key terms**
Cardiovascular fitness: the ability to exercise the entire body for long periods of time.

Flexibility is an aspect of health-related exercise which is often neglected and taken for granted until, for instance, we suddenly cannot bend down easily to tie our shoelaces. It is nonetheless important both in sport and in everyday life. It is most often demonstrated by athletes such as gymnasts, but those who play racket games such as badminton also need to be flexible.

Yoga is an activity which can help to improve flexibility. It is popular with people of all ages, many of whom do not take an active part in other sports.

Body composition is influenced by genetics, although it can be improved by exercise and diet. Some aspects of body composition, such as height, are clearly genetic. Elite athletes work hard to achieve a good body composition for their sport. Body composition is important for everyone. Taking part in physical activity and sport can enhance body shape if a well planned and controlled personal exercise programme (PEP) is followed.

Amir Khan in 2004 (top left) and in 2008 (top right). He is a perfect example of how exercise and diet can impact on body composition.

Weight is usually the first thing people think of in connection with their body composition. The most common and easiest way to get an idea of your body composition is by calculating your body mass index (BMI). This is done by dividing weight in kilograms by height in metres squared (kg/m^2). The result is then checked against a table.

This method is used by the NHS and often by insurance companies to see if applicants for life insurance policies are a safe risk, i.e. they are a healthy weight for their height. Calculating BMI may not give a true result where people are still growing.

Andrew Sheridan weighs over 19st so has a high BMI rating, but this is largely due to muscle.

edexcel :: key terms
Flexibility: the range of movement possible at a joint.

edexcel :: key terms
Body composition: the percentage of body weight that is fat, muscle and bone.

LINK IT UP!

See topic 1.2.1 on diet and somatotypes, for more information on the importance of body composition.

Apply it!

Task 1 – Body Mass Index
Find the heights and weights of two famous sportsmen and two sportswomen, preferably include your role model, and calculate their Body Mass Index.

Discuss the results with the others in your group.

Task 2 – Desirable body weight according to frame size.
Measure your wrist size and see where you are on the table.

Frame	Men	Women
Small	6 inches or less	5.5 or less
Medium	6.25 – 7.25	5.75
Large	7.5 or more	6 or more

Which method is likely to give the most accurate result? Why?

Health-related exercise aspects are usually needed in combination, but not necessarily all at once or in equal amounts. Marathon runners do not need muscular strength but do need muscular endurance. Good flexibility in their lower body will help them to have a good stride length. They will also probably have slim body composition, but the main and essential feature is a high level of cardiovascular fitness to enable them to keep running (exercising) for a very long period of time and at a good pace.

Apply it!

1. Make a note of your favourite activity. Now list the relevant health-related fitness aspects in order of importance.

2. Explain how each aspect is involved in the activity.

Activity	
Football	
Health-related exercise	Explain how used
C/V fitness	
Flexibility	

edexcel ▦ examiner tip

When the question is about health-related exercise, visualise the diagram for health-related exercise and put the names of the five terms on the examination paper at the side of the question. Then choose which of the terms is required to answer the question.

ResultsPlus
Exam Question Report

Long distance runners need high levels of muscular endurance for their event. Explain the term muscular endurance. (1 mark, June 2008)

Answer

An acceptable answer would have been, "the ability to use the muscles many times without getting tired"

How students answered

54% of students got this wrong

Students need to know and to be able to explain what each aspect of health-related exercise is as it is a fundamental part of the specification. Don't make the mistake of getting the explanations of muscular endurance and muscular strength mixed up.

54% 0 marks

Only 46% of students got this right, correctly identifying that muscular endurance is being able to use the muscles repeatedly without getting unduly tired.

46% 1 mark

9: The six components of skill-related fitness

Objectives

Learn about the six components of skill-related fitness and be able to define them:

- ⦾ agility
- ⦾ balance
- ⦾ coordination
- ⦾ power
- ⦾ reaction time
- ⦾ speed

and be able to identify the importance of each to different physical activities.

The last chapter on health-related exercise covered five aspects that you need to know and learn about. This topic, skill-related fitness (sometimes also referred to as motor skills), has six terms.

- ⦿ **A** – Agility
- ⦿ **B** – Balance
- ⦿ **C** – Coordination
- ⦿ **P** – Power
- ⦿ **R** – Reaction Time
- ⦿ **S** – Speed

Skill-related fitness helps people to become good at physical activity. Fitness skills can be developed and improved with practice and training. Different sports need different skills or in many cases a different combination of skills. Being good at more technical activities and events requires more of the six skills.

edexcel ⠿ key terms

Agility: the ability to change the position of the body quickly and to control the movement of the whole body.

Agility means changing direction at speed. Running a 100 metre race does not require agility but doing a floor work exercise in gymnastics does. Imagine a gymnast performing flic-flacs and somersaults – they will need to be very agile. A rugby player running for the try line needs agility to dodge a defender who is trying to tackle him.

edexcel ⠿ examiner tip

The first three terms are easy to remember because they are the first three letters of the alphabet. It might help you to remember the others if you make up a mnemonic such as Peter Power, Robert Reaction Time, and Sarah Speed. In the examination, to avoid getting them mixed up, you could put the six letters at the side of the question on skill-related fitness first.

ResultsPlus
Watch out!

⦿ It is important to understand the difference between health-related and skill-related fitness. If you get these terms mixed up, you could lose vital marks in the exam.

edexcel key terms

Balance: the ability to retain the centre of mass (gravity) of the body above the base of support with reference to static (stationary), or dynamic (changing) conditions of movement, shape and orientation.

Balance

Balance can mean balance while at rest or when on the move.

- Static balance is keeping the body stable while stationary, for instance doing a handstand or the tree position in yoga. Archery and clay pigeon shooting are sports in which static balance is needed.

- Dynamic balance is maintaining a controlled stable position while moving. Hammer throwing and basketball are examples of sports where dynamic balance is essential.

- Both types of balance are needed in some sports, e.g. in gymnastics where a gymnast could be holding a balance, such as a handstand, on the beam (static balance) or keeping balanced while on the move, e.g. a walk-over (dynamic balance).

Holding positions in yoga is an example of static balance

Apply it!

For one of your chosen practical activities, give an example and explain how you would use a static balance. For the same sport or one of your other sports give an example and explain when you would perform a dynamic balance.

edexcel key terms

Coordination: the ability to use two or more body parts together.

Coordination

Just as there are different types of balance there are different types of coordination. Racket games require good hand-eye coordination in order to strike the ball or shuttle correctly.

In football there are several types of coordination.

- Hand-eye coordination for the goalkeeper to catch a shot on goal or catch or punch the ball when it is crossed, often under pressure from the opposition forwards which makes it even more difficult.

- Foot-eye coordination needed to strike the ball to pass, shoot or control it.

Apply it!

Work with a partner to devise a practice in one of your practical activities to improve your coordination. This should be to improve your skill not to test it.

After devising the practice try it out on another pair and let them try their practices out on you. Discuss and compare the success of each practice and think of ways to improve them.

- Head-eye coordination needed to strike the ball with the head in order to clear a corner or to aim at the target to score.

- At other times players may need chest-eye or thigh-eye coordination to control the ball, so coordination is a high priority skill.

Most people tend to be better coordinated on one side of their body than the other – they are better with their right hand than their left, or better with their right foot than their left. Generally, people who are right-handed are right-footed and vice versa, but not always. Some people may be naturally right-handed but left-footed. In some sports, such as cricket, they may even bat right-handed and bowl left-handed. For example, Stuart Broad, an England cricketer, is a right-arm bowler but bats left-handed.

Jonny Wilkinson's winning dropkick in the 2003 World Cup was with his right foot. He can use both feet comfortably, but is naturally left-sided.

edexcel examiner tip

In the exam, when asked to select the skill being shown e.g. in a photograph, and explain how it is being used, go for the most obvious and think of the body using two or more body parts together. In the picture of the crieter, the two body parts are the hands and the eyes (hand-eye coordination). Therefore it is easy to explain how this skill is being used.

Choosing a different skill may make answering the second part of the question more difficult.

Apply it!

Write down the names of two activities in which you participate and explain how coordination is used in each. Try not to choose the same sports as those used above!

edexcel key terms

Power: the ability to undertake strength performances quickly. Power = strength x speed.

Power

Power increases as a result of an increase in strength or speed. Sportsmen or women may use power to propel themselves and/or to propel an object. For instance, sprinters need to be powerful in order to drive their bodies out of the starting blocks when the gun fires to start the race. In athletics, throwers need to be powerful, but they also need to move fast across the circle. Football players take a long throw-in which needs strength and speed but also power at the moment they throw the ball.

In many sports, players need to be able to jump high, either in a game or in high jump or pole vault in athletics. Long jump and triple jump, although they are horizontal jumps, both require power, e.g. at the moment of take-off.

Apply it!

Give an example from one of your sports activities where power is used and explain at what point it is used.

40

edexcel ⊞ key terms
Reaction time: the time between the presentation of a stimulus and the onset of movement.

Reaction tIme

Reaction time is the time between the trigger being pulled, the gun firing and the athletes starting to run. This is the example most people would recognise, the stimulus being the sound of the starting gun, but there are many other examples too. For sprinters it is the time taken to hear the stimulus (sound), but not so for the timekeepers.

The gun fires, the smoke appears, the timekeepers start their watches; for them, the stimulus is the sight of the smoke, not the sound of the gun.

A sight stimulus is the signal for a reaction in most sports. A ball or shuttle is struck and the receiver has to react to the sight; badminton players practise behind screens so they cannot see the shuttlecock and have to react as it comes over the screen. It is possible to measure reactions and improve them through practice. Anticipation from experience can also help reaction time.

Apply it!

Name one of your activities, give an example and explain how reaction time is used. Do not use the examples already given.

edexcel ⊞ key terms
Speed: the differential rate at which an individual is able to perform a movement or cover a distance in a period of time.

Speed

Speed includes:

◉ leg speed, e.g. Usain Bolt

◉ hand speed, e.g. boxer Joe Calzaghe

◉ speed of thought, e.g. tennis star Rafael Nadal.

If a sportsperson could choose just one natural skill-related factor to be a champion it would probably be speed. In some sports a lack of speed can be overcome, but it is an essential ingredient for most champions and it can sometimes make up for a lack of other skills. Mohammed Ali, voted BBC Sports Personality of the Century, boasted that he was so fast he could switch off the light and be in bed before it got dark.

Speed can be improved with practice, e.g. by practising faster leg speed (cadence) and arm movements when sprinting on the spot.

In Summary

Improving skill-related fitness can help improve performance in normal daily work and leisure activities, and can help in the leading of a full, healthy and energetic lifestyle. The same applies to health-related exercise. For example, having good reaction time is useful when driving a car, while good balance is helpful when standing on a chair reaching for something on a high shelf.

Also, it is important to remember how skills relate to each other. For example, in football foot-eye coordination is needed, but so is speed to get to the ball quickly; strength to hold off an opponent; power to get a hard shot on goal and, for goalkeepers, hand-eye coordination and agility to try to save the shot. Think about the hammer throw. This is a technically difficult event where athletes have to:

- swing the hammer above their head while standing still in a controlled position

- rotate on one foot while accelerating across the circle, getting quicker with each turn while maintaining the movement and position of the hammer

- on reaching the front of the circle, launch the hammer with great force at exactly the right moment.

In this series of movements can you indicate where each skill-related factor is being used? Try to think of at least one health-related factor that would also apply.

Look back through this topic for help answering the question.

Apply it!

Make a note of your practical activity you take part in. Make a list of the skill-related fitness aspects that you think are involved in it.

Activity	
Football	
Skill-related fitness	Explain how used
Speed	
Agility	

examzone

Know Zone
Topic 1.1.3: Exercise and fitness as part of your healthy, active lifestyle

Most people who take part in physical activity do so to stay healthy and for the benefits of exercise. To improve fitness and performance requires more specific training that focuses on such aspects as muscular strength, flexibility, agility and speed. Each individual activity requires a number of these but performers also need to be very strong at one or two to be successful.

You should know...

☐ Understand the terms:
- health
- fitness
- exercise
- and understand how they relate to performance in physical activities and a healthy lifestyle

☐ Know and understand the components of health related exercise:
- cardiovascular fitness
- muscular strength
- muscular endurance
- flexibility
- body composition
- and understand how they relate to different physical activities

☐ Know about the six components of skill-related fitness and be able to define them:
- agility
- balance
- coordination
- power
- reaction time
- speed
- and be able to identify the importance of each to different individual physical activities.

Key terms

Health	Body composition
Exercise	Agility
Fitness	Balance
Performance	Coordination
Cardiovascular fitness	Power
Muscular strength	Reaction time
Muscular endurance	Speed
Flexibility	

Which key words match the following definitions?

A The ability to change the position of the body quickly and to control the movement of the whole body.

B The range of movement possible at a joint.

C The differential rate at which an individual is able to perform a movement or cover a distance in a period of time.

D The ability to do strength performances quickly (power = strength x speed).

Examiner's tip
Candidates frequently forget which terms are related to health-related exercise and which are related to skill-related fitness. This problem often leads to a number of lost marks in the exam so make sure you can group them. The first three terms of skill-related fitness are easy to remember because they are the first three letters of the alphabet. It might help you to remember the others if you make up a mnemonic such as Peter Power, Robert Reaction Time, and Sarah Speed. You could do the same for health-related fitness too.

Question: Agility is more important to games players than sprinters. (3 marks)

◯ (i) Explain the term agility. (1)

Students' answer	Build a better answer
A) To be able to change direction with as little difficulty as possible **B)** The ability to change direction travelling at high speed e.g. football player changing the angle of his run to beat a defender	**Student A** does mention a change of direction but it could be changing direction slowly so it gets no marks. (0 marks) **Student B** gives an an excellent answer not only with the explanation – mentioning changing direction at speed - but also providing an example. (1 mark)

▢ (ii) Give a specific example when a games player would use agility during a match. (1)

A) In football a player would need agility to dribble the ball past someone **B)** A rugby player to sidestep a defender	**Student A** would not get a mark because there is no mention of a change of direction. The footballer could dribble past somebody in a straight. (0 marks) **Student B**'s use of the word sidestep is important, as it shows that a change of direction has taken place. (1 mark)

△ (iii) Explain why agility is not important to a 100m sprinter. (1)

A) Because they just need speed to get from start to finish as quick as possible **B)** The 100m sprint track is a straight line from start to finish it does not require athlete to change direction	Once again **Student A** provides no mention of a change of direction. They even fail to say that a 100m runner travels in a straight line which would be a suitable alternative. (0 marks) This is an excellent answer from **Student B** as it mentions both running in a straight line and no change of direction. (1 mark)

Examiner's comment

Student B does well in this question because he clearly understands and states the change in direction at speed that sums up agility. Student A fails to make this clear in their answers which mean he scores no marks. You must be clear about the definitions of all the aspects of HRE and SRF before going into the exam.

Practice Exam Questions

1 Coordination is:

A How well a task is completed

B The ability to use two or more body parts together

C The ability to change position quickly and with control

D Working together as a team
(1 mark)

2 Select a different component of skill-related fitness to complete each of the following statements:

(i) A high jumper needs.....at take off to achieve the height to clear the bar. (1)

(ii) Racket players need.....to move the hand holding the racket to the right place to strike the ball correctly. (1)

(iii) Footballers need.....to beat their opponents to the ball. (1)

(iv) A gymnast needs.....to maintain her position on a beam. (1)
(Total 4 marks)

3 The flexibility of a footballer helps him to achieve the required position to strike the ball.

(i) Explain the term flexibility. (1)

(ii) Name ONE other component of health related exercise that will be important to a footballer's success in striking a ball. (1)

(iii) Explain how the component of health-related exercise you stated will help a footballer's performance. (1) (Total 3 marks)

Topic 1.1.4: Physical activity as part of your healthy, active lifestyle

Sport in Context

Whatever your sport or physical activity, fitness is key. A number of fitness tests, principles and methods of training can be used to measure or improve specific aspects of fitness. In some sports, fitness probably accounts for the difference between the top players and those on the next rung down on the ladder. Different sports require different types of fitness: Chris Hoy, the Olympic cyclist, and Tom Daley, the Olympic diver, have very different needs and very different training programmes.

Training is key to fitness and success. In this topic you will learn the principles and methods of training to consider. Experiencing each method of training will help you apply this knowledge and feel confident about devising your own personal exercise programme (PEP).

PE and me

1. What would you assess before planning a training programme, and how might you test it?

2. Why do you train? Why do you think other people train?

3. How would you get the most out of a training programme?

4. What do you do before and after a training session or game?

Topic Overview

By the end of this topic you should:

- assess fitness levels and apply the principles of training when constructing a personal exercise programme
- understand that there are a number of training methods and be able to explain the benefits of each one
- describe a 'typical' training session.

10: Assessing your fitness levels

Objectives

At the end of this chapter you should:

○ know what is meant by a PAR-Q

○ be able to assess health-related exercise, and skill-related fitness using a number of tests.

Personal readiness, PAR-Q (Physical Activity Readiness Questionnaire)

Before starting an exercise programme you must make sure you are ready to do so. You should go to see your doctor and have a medical examination – especially if you have been in poor health, had an injury, or a virus infection, or if you are getting over a cold or flu. There are several standard questions (a questionnaire) that you also need to ask yourself.

Before you can complete the questionnaire you need to be sure about your medical history: any medical conditions, respiratory problems or other concerns. You should also be quite clear about your previous sporting or exercise history. The questions you should consider are:

1. Have you any medical conditions e.g. a heart condition?

2. Do you experience chest pains?

3. Do you have any ongoing injuries?

4. Do you have high or low blood pressure?

5. Do you have diabetes?

6. Do you have asthma?

7. Have you had a cold or flu or a virus in the last four weeks?

8. Is there any other reason why you should not do physical activity?

If you honestly answered NO to all the questions above, and you're happy with your current medical condition, then you can start and then gradually increase your level of physical activity.

Exercises to assess fitness levels

Before starting an exercise programme you should have decided what you are aiming to improve. You could look at the five aspects of health-related exercise (HRE) and the six aspects of skill-related fitness (SRF).

Before starting the programme it will be very helpful to test the aspects of HRE or SRF that you want to improve. This will give you a starting point for your programme – a benchmark against which you can measure yourself at the end of it – which will then show whether you have improved the areas of fitness or skill you set out to enhance.

edexcel ::: examiner tip

It is important to follow what is known as the 'correct protocol'. This refers to the set way of doing the test. If you do it one way and then re-do the test another way the test will not be valid, and your scores will not be accurate against any scoring table.

You will look at a number of tests in two groups. Some people may only choose to do the ones related to the aspects they want to improve. Others may do them all and then decide which aspects of HRE and SRF they need to improve in their programme.

At the end of these tests you should:

○ know what you are testing

○ know whether it is a health-related or skill-related test.

Health-related exercise fitness tests

Cooper's 12-minute run test

This tests cardiovascular fitness and muscular endurance in a participant's legs. Participants run round a course for 12 minutes. They then measure the distance covered and calculate their VO2 max (aerobic capacity). This test can also be performed on a treadmill.

Hand grip strength test

Tests muscular strength in the hand. Take a hand grip dynamometer and squeeze as tightly as possible. Take three recordings. Record the best score.

Sit and reach flexibility test

This test measures the flexibility of the harmstrings. Either use a standard sit and reach box or sit down with legs straight and feet against a bench set on its side. Measure how far beyond your toes you can reach. Somebody who cannot reach their toes scores a minus total. If you just reach your toes you score zero, which is average.

Harvard step test

This test measures cardiovascular endurance and muscular endurance. Step on and off a bench – which should be at a height of 45 cms – every 2 seconds for 5 minutes. Keep to a regular pace so that you step on and off once every 2 seconds, making 150 steps in 5 minutes (30 steps a minute). It may help to count 1 – 2 – 3 – 4 for a complete step on and off the bench. Take your pulse at 1, 2 and 3 minutes into recovery, to measure your heart's rate of recovery. The fitter you are the quicker the recovery.

Step ups

Skill-related fitness tests

Illinois agility run

This test assesses agility. A course is set like the one in the diagram. Participants are required to run around and change direction on numerous occasions. The run is timed, and the aim is to complete the tests as quickly as possible.

Physical	Males 15–16 yrs	Females 15–16 yrs
High score	Faster than 15.9s	Faster than 17.5s
Above average	15.9–16.7s	17.5–18.6s
Average	16.8–18.6s	18.2–22.4s
Below average	18.7–18.8s	22.4–23.4s
Low score	Slower than 18.8s	Slower than 23.4s

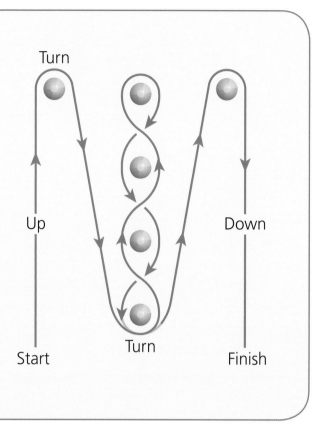

Turn

Up   Down

Start   Turn   Finish

Standing stork test

The stork test measures a person's balance (static). Stand on both feet, put your hands on your hips, lift one leg and put your foot on the knee of the other leg. Time how long you can hold this position. You must keep the foot on the knee and the heel of the standing foot off the ground. Repeat the test on the other foot. Re-test after training to improve your balance and analyse against your original score.

Performers about to go up on to their toes

Gender	Excellent	Above Average	Average	Below	Poor
Male	>50 secs	50 – 41 secs	40 – 31 secs	Average 30 – 20 secs	<20 secs
Female	>30 secs	30 – 23 secs	22 – 16 secs	15 – 10 secs	<10 secs

Sergeant jump test

This tests leg power. Chalk your finger tips and touch the wall as high as you can. Bend your knees and jump, touching the wall at the highest point of the jump. Measure how high above your standing reach mark you jumped and record your result. Score the best of three attempts.

Standing broad jump

This test also measures power. Measure your height on the floor by lying down and getting somebody to mark where your feet are, and where your head is. From a standing jump, at the marker for your feet, see how far beyond your own height you can jump. Score the best of three attempts.

Ruler drop test

This tests reaction time. Work with a partner. Your partner holds a 1 metre ruler at 0 cm. You place your thumb and forefinger of your preferred hand at the 50 cm mark. Your partner decides when to release the ruler. Your must catch the ruler between the thumb and forefinger as quickly as possible. Measure the distance it took to catch the ruler.

Score
Over 42 cm = excellent
37–42 cm = good
29–37 cm = average
22–29 cm = fair
Below 22 cm = poor

30-metre sprint

This tests a person's speed. Mark out a 30 metre distance. When you are signalled to start, run as fast as you can. A partner needs to record your time. (This can also be done over different distances.)

Three ball juggle

Juggling tests coordination. Using three tennis balls juggle for as long as you can without dropping a ball or stopping. A partner should time you.

After working through these tests you should have a list of results. You can use your exercise programme to work towards improving these.

Apply it!

Without looking at the information above choose a test that is suitable for each aspect of health-related exercise and one which is suitable for skill-related fitness.

11: The principles of training

Objectives

By the end of this topic you will be able to:

- explain the principles of training – individual needs, progressive overload, specificity, rest and recovery, the FITT principle, and reversibility
- show how to use these principles to improve your fitness and/or skills in a personal exercise programme
- explain the components of the FITT principle (frequence, intensity, time and type) and understand how components overlap with other principles of training
- appreciate how application of the FITT principle can improve performance and fitness
- understand the term reversibility and its impact on performance.

You have already learned how to assess your personal levels of fitness before starting an exercise programme. This section looks at the principles of training and how to use them:

- individual needs / differences
- specificity
- progressive overload
- rest and recovery.

Individual needs/differences

When planning a personal exercise programme (PEP) individual needs must be taken into account. Using someone else's personal exercise programme will not work because every athlete has different needs, and training should be focused on these. For example, athletes starting out a programme with a very low level of fitness should not follow someone else's programme who has been training for a long time. They may find this too difficult and give up, or they may even sustain an injury.

An extreme example would be a first time marathon runner using an experienced marathon runner's training programme. The first time marathon runner would not have the level of fitness, experience or motivation to benefit from it and could potentially risk injuring themselves.

To use individual needs in a personal exercise programme you would take into account your body build, the sport (and position played) and your aims.

Specificity

Specificity means matching training to the requirements of an activity. Every sport has its own specialist needs; divers and long-distance runners obviously train differently. Specificity in football might mean concentrating on cardiovascular fitness (health-related exercise) or speed (skill-related fitness). The first enables players to keep going for longer, while the second helps them to move quickly during a game. Goalkeepers, on the other hand, have different training needs (agility) and premiership football clubs have specialist goalkeeper coaches.

The need for specificity is clear in a game such as rugby where the players must be very fit and strong. However, the forwards need to train for strength when pushing in the scrum while the backs need to be fast and agile to get past the defenders.

Using specificity in a personal exercise programme

In your personal exercise programme you could use the principle of specificity by training to improve your cardiovascular fitness, and choosing particular methods of training to do this. This should be made clear in your PEP and where highlighted you are using the principle of specificity.

Apply it!

1. In some sports there are different positions that call for different fitness requirements. Name a sport where this is the case and state which health-related exercise and which skill-related fitness aspects need to be trained.

2. Write down three different physical activities that have similar fitness needs. Mention Specific positions if this is relevant. Think about how the principle of specificity applies to these activities.

ResultsPlus
Watch out!

● The word is SPECIFICITY. Some students use specify, special, specific, or even specification. You must use the correct word and spell it correctly.

Progressive overload

This means gradually increasing the amount of overload so as to gain fitness without the risk of injury.

Overload describes when an athlete trains more than they normally do. This is the only way athletes can improve their fitness. It is often mistaken for training too much, or training too hard, but this is not correct. It means working at a higher range of intensity than the minimum required to improve fitness (the minimum threshold of training) while staying below the maximum (the maximum threshold of training). This is known as the target zone. You will learn more about this later in CH16.

The principle of **progressive overload** i.e. gradually increasing the amount of overload applies to all areas of health-related exercise. For example, overload training for muscular strength may mean lifting a weight at 60 to 80 per cent of maximum effort. For muscular endurance, between 60 and 80 per cent of maximum repetitions might be classed as overload training. Overload training to improve flexibility means that the stretch must reach the end of the full range of movement. This point must be reached or passed in order to bring about improvement.

Improving cardiovascular fitness means reducing resting heart rate. How overload training applies to cardiovascular fitness is covered later in this topic.

Using progressive overload in a personal exercise programme

A six-week personal exercise programme should be reviewed and evaluated after about two weeks. Overload can then gradually be increased and the programme reviewed again after another two weeks. In this way, training loads are gradually adjusted using **progressive overload**.

ResultsPlus
Watch out!

- Overload does not mean training too hard or too much. This is a common mistake in the exam.

Rest and recovery

- Rest: the period of time allotted to recovery.

- Recovery: the time required to repair damage to the body caused by training or competition.

The human body is very clever; it reacts to a hard training session by increasing its ability to cope with future punishing training sessions. This is called adaptation. However, the body recovers and adaptation takes place while at rest.

Using rest and recovery in a personal exercise programme

Rest must be included in a personal exercise programme to allow time for recovery and adaptation.

For example, someone training five times a week would probably train on three days, take a day off to recover (and allow adaptation to take place), then train on the next two days and rest again on the seventh. Professionals may follow a programme where they train more often than this, but they may rest different parts of their bodies on different days.

54

The FITT principle

The FITT principle is used to guide you in planning an exercise programme to get the most out of it as safely as possible. The FITT principle works with the principle of progressive overload because as you get fitter you can train more frequently; train at a higher intensity; and/or train at a higher intensity for longer periods of time at a given type of activity.

FITT stands for:

◉ frequency

◉ intensity

◉ time

◉ type.

Frequency means planning how often to train. It can be used to regulate progressive overload. For example, frequency should be a minimum of three times a week, but could be increased to four times a week. Frequency overlaps with the principles of rest and recovery, and can be used to make good use of these. For example, training every other day would allow a rest to recover on the days between training. This would give the body time to adapt and gain the benefits from the training session.

Intensity means how hard someone trains. This overlaps with the principle of progressive overload. Intensity might vary depending on the aims and type of training. However, whatever the type of training, it must be carried out at a worthwhile level of intensity. Planning the intensity of training correctly is very important.

Time means how long each training session must last in order to be of any benefit and to achieve improvement.

◉ At least 20 minutes per session should be spent in the target zone. This does not mean five minutes to warm up, five to train, five to cool-down and another five to shower and change back again!

◉ In terms of cardiovascular fitness, at least 20 minutes should be spent training with the pulse in the target zone after a good warm-up and before a proper cool-down.

Professionals will train for much longer than this to reach their required levels of fitness. They will probably spend more than 20 minutes just warming up and marathon runners are likely to spend a little over two hours running 20 miles on a Sunday morning, in addition to all the other training they do during the week.

Apply it!

The principle of frequency overlaps with the principle of rest and recovery. Can you explain how?

Type means the method(s) of training chosen to achieve a person's particular goals. Type overlaps with the principle of specificity; training should be chosen according to what needs to be improved and what the end goal is. If strength needs to be improved by training, is it muscular strength or muscular endurance? If cardiovascular fitness, is it for a particular sport or physical activity?

Many people may want to improve their overall fitness without having a particular goal in mind. This could be achieved through a wide variety of activities which raise the pulse rate into the target zone to maintain a healthy active lifestyle – such activities could include dancing (from disco to line to ballroom), as well as swimming, cycling, brisk walking, jogging, aerobics, using the cross trainer, and so on.

The type of training is more important for sportspeople who specialise in one event and want to compete at a high level. For example, sprinters train specifically to improve their speed.

Apply it!

Write down three ways that could increase the intensity of a training session.

Reversibility

Reversibility means gradually losing fitness instead of progressing or remaining at the current level. This happens when a person is ill or injured. Some people keep their fitness longer than others; this may be related to how long they have taken to build up their fitness or how serious their illness or injury was. However, anyone will lose fitness if they stop training. This is a principle of training you do not want to use.

Apply it!

One way to measure both progression and reversibility is to take your pulse rate after completing your training programme, and then measure how long it takes for your pulse to get back to normal.

edexcel ▦ key terms

Individual differences/needs: matching training to the requirements of an individual.

Specificity: matching training to the requirements of an activity.

Progressive overload: to gradually increase the amount of overload so that fitness gains occur, but without potential for injury.

Rest: the period of time allotted to recovery.

Recovery: the time required for the repair of damage to the body caused by training or competition.

FITT: Frequency, intensity, time, type (used to increase the amount of work the body does, in order to achieve overload).

Reversibility: any adaptation that takes place as a consequence of training will be reversed when you stop training.

Apply it!

Specific: your goals in your personal exercise programme will almost certainly be linked to the testing you did earlier. For example, you might want to run 100 metres further in your Cooper's Run test.

Measurable: running 100 metres further in your Cooper's Run test can be measured.

Achievable: an extra 100 metres is achievable if you train properly for six weeks.

Realistic: an extra 100 metres after six weeks is a realistic goal.

Time-bound: you have set the end of your six-week programme as your goal, so it is time-bound, i.e. you have six weeks to achieve it.

Congratulations, you have set SMART goals!

LINK IT UP!

The tests which you might have performed from CH10 should help you to evaluate your current levels before setting your goals.

edexcel ::: examiner tip

SMART: specific – measurable – achievable – realistic – time-bound.
You need to be able to explain these words and use them in setting goals for your own personal exercise programme.

People who run in the London Marathon come from very different backgrounds: the star athletes have been training for years and know exactly what they are trying to achieve and how, as do many of the good club athletes, although at a lower level. The first-time marathon runner has little idea what is involved in preparing for and running the marathon. The overall goal of 'I want to complete the London Marathon' may be too daunting. It is useful for such runners to make smaller specific goals, such as running increasing distances, building up to the end goal of being able to run the London Marathon distance of 26 miles and 385 yards (42.195 km).

13: Methods of training

Objectives

By the end of these pages you should be able to:

- know and describe the six different training methods: interval, continuous, Fartlek, circuit, weight, and cross
- know which sports and activities each is most suited to
- explain how each can improve health and fitness
- understand their relationships with the components of fitness and principles of training.

There are six different training methods:

- interval
- continuous
- fartlek
- circuit
- weight
- cross.

Learning these training methods is easiest if you actually experience each one as this will help you to apply your knowledge.

Fitness is very important to all physical activities. In some sports, fitness probably makes the difference between players at the highest level and the rest. A number of training methods can be used to improve fitness. Each is designed for a specific purpose, to improve a specific aspect of fitness, and therefore each suits different sports and activities.

ResultsPlus
Watch out!

It is easy to confuse training method and the principles of training. Be careful!

Interval training

Interval training is suitable for many different sports, from individual activities such as swimming and athletics to team games such as football and hockey. It may be better for team players, as it fits the style of many games, with short bursts followed by slow walking or jogging or stopping. Interval training is defined as high intensity periods of work followed by defined periods of rest. It is possible to train individually, with a partner, or in a team or group. The aim of interval training is to have a high intensity, quality workout.

The 'work' period, or interval, may be a distance to run, such as 60 metres, or a time to run, such as 10 seconds. This factor will probably be linked in some way to the particular activity, using the principle of specificity.

LINK IT UP!

Sprinters who use interval training to improve their speed are also using the principle of specificity, since they have chosen this specific training method to improve their performance. Turn to CH11 to remind yourself of the principle of specificity.

LINK IT UP!

The 'rest' interval links back to the principles of rest and recovery that you looked at earlier in CH11. Controlling the length of the 'rest' interval allows participants to work at a higher intensity in the workout which links back to the FITT principle in CH12.

The 'rest' period, or interval, may be a walk back to the starting point, or simply not working (rest). The duration of this should be at least 30 seconds to allow recovery and to be ready for the next work interval, otherwise the quality, or intensity, of the work is not likely to be good enough.

The number of repetitions of work and rest periods is important in interval training. One repetition is equal to one work period plus one rest period. For example, this might be one run of 60 metres followed by a 30-second rest period. A set (of repetitions) may be four, five or six runs of 60 metres, each with a 30-second rest period. An athlete may perform a number of sets with longer rest intervals between the sets; for example, four sets, with each set consisting of four repetitions of 60 metre sprints with a walk back as the rest interval between repetitions, and then three minutes rest between sets.

Advantages of interval training

Interval training is mainly designed to improve speed, but will also improve cardiovascular fitness; it is high intensity and always done at a fast pace.

- It includes repeated sprint running or swimming, which is anaerobic.

- It includes a rest period (interval) which allows recovery.

- Heart rates can be measured and shown in graphic form, so they can be evaluated and the quality of the sessions compared.

- It takes place over short periods or bursts.

- It includes repetitions of high quality work which raise the pulse rate to near maximum. This will improve cardiovascular fitness.

LINK IT UP!

To revise what cardiovascular fitness is, turn to CH 8

Continuous training

Continuous training is steady training. The working heart rate will not be very high (intensity), there are no rest periods, and a session usually lasts for at least 15 to 20 minutes. Continuous training may be the most suitable to improve cardiovascular endurance for a sedentary adult who has not trained for some time and is quite unfit. It is appropriate where high intensity exercise may be unwise. It may take various forms and could start with brisk walking, graduating to jogging.

Although interval training may be more suitable for games which involve short bursts of activity followed by slow walking or jogging (such as football), continuous training may be more appropriate at the start of the season, or during the off-season. Long-distance athletes, cyclists, and swimmers may use continuous training as it resembles their actual competitive activity. However, they are more likely to use a combination of both interval, continuous, and fartlek.

Apply it!

1. Walk briskly for 15 minutes, on your own or with a partner whose fitness level is similar. Check your starting and finishing points. How far do you think you walked?

This may be a good way to start training after injury or after a long lay-off.

2. On your own or with the same partner, start from the same point and try to jog continuously for seven minutes over the same course. How close are you to the finishing point of your walk? How far do you think you have run?

Which session did you find the hardest?

Advantages of continuous training

- Improves aerobic fitness, as it includes long, comparatively slow, activity.
- It is very cheap, apart from the cost of suitable footwear in the case of running.
- Can be done individually or in a group.
- It is suitable for improving health and fitness.
- Can be done in a variety of places.
- Can be adapted to individual needs and to use the FITT principle.
- A wide range of activities can be used, including running, jogging, swimming, cycling, as well as exercise machines such as rowing machines, exercise bicycles, treadmills, cross trainers, and skiing machines.
- Can be adapted using the FITT principle.

Day	am	pm
Monday	Five miles easy – continuous run	Eight miles brisk – continuous run
Tuesday	Six miles fartlek – several three-minute bursts up hill	Rest
Wednesday	Five miles easy – continuous run	10 miles fartlek with six x 4-minute hill runs
Thursday	Eight miles continuous run	Rest
Friday	Five miles easy – continuous run	Five miles jog – continuous run
Saturday	Rest	Rest or race
Sunday	20–22 miles continuous run	Rest

An example of a week's training for a good marathon runner.

Fartlek training

Fartlek training is suitable for games such as football, netball, and hockey, because it includes the short bursts of activity – such as starting and stopping and fast sprinting followed by a short rest – which are typical of these games.

Fartlek training originated in Sweden. The word fartlek is a combination of the two Swedish words for 'speed' and 'play'. Fartlek is a combination of fast and slow running and predates interval training. In Scandinavia it was originally carried out in the countryside in pleasant terrain and often included running up hills.

In many ways fartlek resembles interval training; like interval training, it includes periods of work followed by periods of rest (or lighter work). However, fartlek sessions include sprints of varying distances, not necessarily measured distances as in interval training. So a session might include a sprint of 200 metres from one tree to another, or up a hill of no measured distance at all.

Apply it!

In a group write a short paragraph or make a table comparing interval training, continuous training and fartlek training, or discuss the similarities and differences. Make sure you are clear about the differences.

edexcel ::: examiner tip

Fartlek and interval training are very similar, so make sure you show in your answer that fartlek takes place over different terrain and can include hills.

Advantages of fartlek training

- Can take place away from the track over pleasant landscapes and terrain.

- Can be done over a variety of terrain, e.g. sand dunes near a beach, parkland and forests.

- Can include hill work, both up and down hills.

- Can include repetitions, e.g. up the same hill several times.

- Programmes can be very flexible.

- Rest periods can be included or the session can be continuous with intermittent hard and easy running.

- It is suited to most games such as rugby and netball, as well as general fitness programmes.

Circuit training

Circuit training primarily improves local muscular endurance, cardiovascular fitness, and circulo-respiratory fitness (i.e. the heart, the blood, the blood vessels and the lungs).

LINK IT UP!

- See Topic 1.1.3, CH 8 for an explanation of muscular endurance within health related exercise, and Topic 1.2.4 which looks at the role of muscles.

- See Topic 1.1.3, CH 8 for an explanation of cardiovascular fitness within health related exercise, and Topic 1.2.2 which looks at the role of the cardiovascular system.

Circuit training involves a number of exercises, arranged so as to avoid exercising the same muscle groups consecutively. Each takes place at an exercise 'station' in a gym or sports hall, or out of doors.

Circuit training develops general fitness, working both the muscles and the cardiovascular system. It is therefore suitable for a wide range of activities, including football and boxing. It is also excellent training for badminton and tennis players: many professional players use circuit training as part of their personal exercise programmes.

Repetitions and circuit training

Exercises at each station may be carried out for a set length of time, e.g. as many repetitions as possible in 30 seconds, or for a set number of times, e.g. 30 repetitions, according to the fitness level of the participant. After completing each set of repetitions, the person training moves on to the next exercise until a whole circuit has been completed. After resting for perhaps two minutes, the circuit is repeated. Usually three circuits are completed in a session.

Some circuit training sessions are quite sophisticated, perhaps using a different number of repetitions for different levels of fitness. These may be colour coded; for example, red for people with low fitness levels, yellow for those with medium fitness levels and green for those with high fitness levels; the high fitness circuit would include more exercises in the set time. Exercises may also be done to high tempo music to motivate and inspire the participants to work harder (higher intensity). The music may be stopped every 30 seconds and re-started after the same length of time or the set rest period. Extra exercises may be added or the rest period shortened to make the circuit harder or to increase the intensity.

Apply it!

Explain how the intensity, from the FITT principle, is applied in circuit training.

Then explain why the order of the exercises is important.

64

Skills circuit

Another way to use circuit training is to have a skills circuit for a particular activity. Instead of doing different exercises at each station, a different skill for the chosen sport is practised. For example, a basketball skills circuit could have dribbling at station 1, chest passes at station 2, jump shooting at station 3, and so on. Notice that these skills have been chosen in a particular order; a chest passing station is not followed by a javelin passing station.
Decide if the circuit is for fitness or skills or a combination of each.

edexcel examiner tip

In the exam you will be expected to be able to design a fitness circuit or a skills circuit or a combination of both.

You may be given an example of a circuit and asked to state its faults and suggest how to improve it.

Think about how the stations are set out. Are the muscle groups being worked consecutively?

LINK IT UP!

Skills circuits effectively apply the principle of specificity.

Advantages of circuit training

Circuit training is better for general all round fitness than interval, continuous or fartlek training. It is very popular and many exercise classes now include this type of work.

- It can combine muscular strength, muscular endurance, agility, coordination, power, speed and cardiovascular fitness effectively within one session.

- The equipment need not be expensive.

- People of all levels of fitness and ability can take part as exercises can be tailored to suit individual needs.

- Includes both aerobic and anaerobic activities.

- Uses a wide range of exercises, which makes the session more interesting.

- People work hard and can be highly motivated to succeed and reach their goals.

- Uses the principle of progressive overload.

Apply it!

1. Note what physical activity you are training for or if you are training to improve your general fitness.

2. Design a fitness training circuit that you are going to use as part of your personal exercise programme, possibly as part of your fitness training unit.

3. Choose six exercises that will improve your all-round fitness. Make sure the circuit is designed so that no two muscle groups are exercised successively. Include a cardiovascular exercise station.

4. Design a gym lay-out which shows all your exercises clearly. Make work cards to explain each exercise, and where possible use a diagram or photograph/s to show the movements. Explain which muscles are being exercised at each station.

5. Explain how the circuit will work e.g. 30 seconds work, 30 seconds recovery, then move to the next station. You could produce a CD with music to motivate and help you work at a higher intensity.

Weight training

Weight training uses progressive resistance, either in the form of the actual weight lifted or in terms of the number of times the weight is lifted (repetitions). It is used to:

1. increase muscular strength

2. increase muscular endurance

3. increase speed

4. develop muscle bulk (size)

5. rehabilitate after illness or injury.

Weight training is suitable for people who take part in strength events in athletics, speed and jumping events such as sprinting and long jump, and rugby.

Constructing a weight training schedule

A weight training schedule is a programme setting out in detail what is to be achieved and how. The principles of training, such as FITT, are used to plan the type of work to be carried out in the programme.

The purpose of the training should be decided first. This will affect.

1. Number of exercises

For someone starting weight training, a selection of 6–8 exercises would probably be suitable. This is known as a core training programme: a set of exercises suitable for general but not specific use. Once the core programme has been completed, the number of exercises based on specific muscles might be increased or decreased.

2. Exercises for each muscle group

In the early stages of weight training, it would be best to follow a core programme set by the teacher/instructor, before concentrating on particular muscle groups. Long jumpers, for example, will work on their leg muscles.

3. Weight used

The safest amount is about 40 to 50 per cent of the five repetition maximum or rep max (RM). One RM is the maximum a person can lift once, so five RM is the most a person can lift five times.

4. Number of repetitions

In the sets method of training it is usual to perform 10 repetitions per set. Experienced athletes might vary repetitions depending on whether they are building muscular strength (fewer repetitions) or muscular endurance (more repetitions).

5. Number of sets

Normally three sets of 10 repetitions are performed, but for the first two weeks of a six-week programme it is probably best to start with two sets and move up to three sets after two weeks. This uses the principle of progressive overload. Again, experienced athletes may vary sets depending on their goals.

6. How fast the exercise is done

It is more important, when starting out, to be in control of the weights than to work too quickly. The repetitions should be done in 1.5 to 2.0 seconds.

7. Length of rest between sets

Recovery between sets is normally about 1–2 minutes. If working with a training partner or partners, taking turns is normally about the same amount of time.

8. Frequency of training

The 'sets method' of weight training (three sets of 10 repetitions) is not so demanding or intensive as pure strength training (which involves heavier weights), so does not need the same amount of rest between sessions. However, at least one rest day between sessions is advisable for novice weight trainers.

Advantages of weight training

◉ Can be used to improve muscular strength, muscular endurance or power depending on how the programme is organised.

◉ There is a wide variety of exercises from which to choose. A programme can be created to improve specific muscle groups, e.g. bench press develops the pectoral muscles.

◉ It is easy to monitor progress and overload.

LINK IT UP!

You might want to revisit the pages on muscular strength and muscular endurance in CH8.

See Principles of Training, rest and recovery in CH11.

Apply it!

Use the information on weight training to construct a weight training schedule of six suitable exercises for your six-week personal exercise programme.

Make work cards with diagrams or pictures for each exercise, as you did with the circuit training. You could have pictures of yourself doing the exercises. Explain which muscle groups are being trained. Are you working to improve muscular strength or muscular endurance?

Cross training

Cross training is a mixture of training. This helps to break up the monotony of using one method and can also help to reduce the stresses on the body which can result from using a single training method. For example, running on hard surfaces every day increases wear on the joints of the lower body.

Cross training can be used to produce the same effects as a single type of training, but through using quite different types of work/play, and, being a mixture of different types of training, can more easily be adapted to suit individual needs. Someone who trains four times a week, for example, may do two sessions of continuous training such as swimming, and two of fartlek training, running outdoors. If an extra session was wanted, a circuit training session in the gym could be added; that would be a week of training using most of the training methods and would result in excellent all round fitness.

This sort of schedule is a good way for most people to maintain a high level of all-round fitness while staying motivated. This type of schedule is also used by many professional sportspeople, as most of them need a combination of health and skill-related fitness factors. Examples might include:

◉ Sprinters need speed, so they use interval training; power and strength, so they use weight training; and they may also use other methods such as circuit training.

◉ Racket players need speed, so they use interval training; they also use circuit training for muscular endurance.

Athletes may also use other methods of training at different times e.g. continuous and/or fartlek for general cardiovascular fitness after their end of season break.

edexcel ⠿ examiner tip

Remember cross training is a combination of training methods, not activities. It does not mean going swimming one day, playing football the next, and badminton the next.

Advantages of cross training

◉ Allows for a variety of training and can therefore make training more interesting.

◉ You can train with different people in different activities, or you can train alone.

◉ Certain muscle groups can be rested from day to day, e.g. continuous on the road one day, interval in the pool on another day, circuit training in the gym on another day, fitting rest and recovery days in between.

◉ Training can be adapted to the weather conditions, e.g. change to swimming in an indoor pool if the weather is poor for running.

Apply it!

Choose and explain how two athletes, for example a sprinter and a marathon runner, would use cross training to prepare for their sport by choosing – from the table below – the two methods of training that each may use. Each athlete must have two different methods from the other.

Methods of Training	
Weight Training	Continuous Training
Interval Training	Circuit Training
Fartlek Training	Cross Training

1

2

3

4

14: The exercise session

Objectives

By the end of this section you should:

○ Understand and be able to explain a warm-up, main activity and cool-down and the importance of each in connection with a training session.

A training session, match, or competition should always be split into three sections which are performed in the same logical order:

◉ warm-up

◉ main activity

◉ cool-down.

The warm-up

The warm-up gradually raises body temperature and heart rate and improves the exchange of oxygen from haemoglobin.

A warm-up is essential to:

1. prevent injury

2. improve performance

3. practise skills before the event / match / game

4. prepare psychologically for the event.

A warm-up should provide a smooth transition from rest to the intensity of the main activity or competitive situation. For example, in football the first sprint should be during the warm-up, not the match! This applies equally to all games players, athletes, and swimmers.

Cardiovascular warm-up

Every training or exercise session or competitive situation should start with a cardiovascular warm-up which gradually raises the heart rate towards the working heart rate. The cardiovascular warm-up can take various forms, depending on the main activity, but can include cycling on a static bicycle (which is often used by rugby teams), skipping, swimming, or more usually easy jogging and walking.

This part of the warm-up usually takes between 5 and 15 minutes depending on the person and the activity. International athletes preparing for a competition would probably take much longer and during this time would also be preparing psychologically. Many use music to help their motivation.

Stretching

Stretching forms the second phase of the warm-up, and there are different ways to do it.

- Static: easy stretches which are held for about 10–15 seconds without straining.
- Dynamic (ballistic): bouncing stretches (not recommended by some coaches).

Stretching is usually performed logically starting at the top of the body (i.e. neck and shoulder stretches) and working down to the ankles and feet. Pay extra attention to those areas used in your sport, i.e. neck and shoulders in rugby.

Static stretching is recommended and should be related to the activity. For example, if the game is football then stretching the gastrocnemius, hamstring and quadriceps is essential, but the goalkeeper would also need to include some specialist exercises, perhaps of a gymnastic nature. A swimmer would include stretches specific to the stroke or strokes that they are about to perform.

Dynamic (ballistic) stretching is not recommended by some coaches, although some athletes use it just before an event, possibly after they have been warming up for a long time using static stretches. In some cases, it may also be part of their psychological preparation (some athletes like to follow the same ritual every time they compete).

Apply it!

Choose an activity, then describe and/or demonstrate to a partner three stretches suitable for that activity. The stretches should:

1. be for different parts of the body
2. start with the upper body and finish with the lower body
3. be static or dynamic stretches.

Explain why the stretches you have described are good for the activity you have chosen.

Specific skills practice

Warming-up should include practising skills specific to the activity. For example, tennis players practise particular shots, such as volleys, forehand and backhand. Cricketers practise catching, bowling, and batting. In football, goalkeepers practise catching crosses and shots and throwing the ball. Sprinters practise sprint starts to get used to driving out of their starting blocks.

The warm-up should finish just before the main activity or event starts.

70

The main activity or event

This is usually a training session using one of the methods of training, although it can also be a game or competition. It always raises the performer's heart rate above the normal level and lasts for at least 20 minutes. It can take various forms, e.g. a continuous training session, depending on the activity and the objective of the training.

- If part of a training session, the main activity could be continuous training for a long distance runner, or a skill circuit for a hockey player.

- The main activity could be taking part in a competitive match, for example in the Premier League.

- In some extreme situations performers may be trying to lose weight, e.g. a boxer training for a world title fight.

- The aim may also be rehabilitation after injury or illness or to improve fitness generally through a personal exercise programme.

Choosing a main activity

The main activity depends on many things. The level at which the performer is training is obviously important; professional athletes are more likely to be doing interval training while fun runners are more likely to be doing continuous runs in preparation for a fun run.

Timing should be taken into account. Is it pre-season or just before a major competition, when training may be lighter and more speed work included? Is the activity aimed at improving cardiovascular fitness, muscular strength, muscular endurance, or flexibility? Is it to be a skills sessions to improve agility perhaps in a circuit, power in the weights room, speed on the track, or a combination of both fitness and skills? Or is the session designed to work on a health-related aspect of fitness? What is the performer's body shape? Running may not be a good option for some people, an exercise bicycle may be better.

LINK IT UP!

To find out more about body types see CH 19.

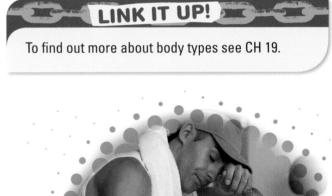

The cool-down

As the warm-up gradually raises heart rate and body temperature to the level necessary for the activity, so the cool-down gradually returns the body to its normal resting heart rate and temperature.

Every training session and competitive situation should finish with a cool-down, and this is most important after an anaerobic work-out. Cooling down properly is important as it disperses lactic acid – a poison – produced during exercise which helps to prevent stiffness and soreness in the muscles.

Activities similar to those used in the warm-up, such as jogging, can be used to return the heart rate gradually to its resting level. The cool-down takes about 5–10 minutes to return the heart rate to normal, depending on the activity. This is usually followed by 10–15 minutes of stretching, although, as with the warm-up, many athletes take much longer than this. The static stretches in the cool-down are held for about 30–35 seconds, and they should start at the top and work systematically downwards.

Relaxation exercises should finish the session, especially if the main activity has been of high intensity. This relaxation should last for 10–15 minutes; quiet music is sometimes used during these exercises. Relaxation exercises could start in a sitting position, with legs crossed as in yoga, with some breathing exercises, and continue lying down flexing and relaxing muscles for 20 seconds, again in sequence starting from the neck and shoulders. In some exercise classes, particularly yoga, participants may be asked while lying down to imagine they are on a nice sandy beach on a lovely sunny day, feeling heavy, relaxed, calm, and peaceful. This helps to relieve stress and tension and leads to a sense of wellbeing – one of the most important benefits of exercise for many people.

15: Comparing two types of training session

Objectives

By the end of these pages you should be able to:

○ understand and explain how a method of training can be used to create different effects and improve physical performance

○ understand how different methods of training can match individual needs and differences

○ use the principle of specificity.

Case study

Jack and Tom are brothers and both do athletics. Jack is a very good 100 metres sprinter and Tom runs the 1500 metres. They both use interval training to improve their performance. However, their sessions are quite different. This is because they apply the principles of specificity and individual needs, the FITT principle, and overload to their own events. This means that they create a session that specifically develops the areas they need to improve if they are to succeed.

After a warm-up suitable for the activity Jack and Tom would complete these training sessions.

LINK IT UP!

You can look back at the elements of a training session i.e. warm-up, main activity, cool-down on the previous pages.

Session A: Jack's training for a 100m sprint

Jack works with a partner, so they can record each other's results. Using a 'rolling start', i.e. from about 20 yards before the start line, Jack gradually builds up speed so that when he crosses the start line, he is at full speed. He then:

1. runs 60 metres at 90 per cent effort – then records his pulse rate

2. walks or slow jogs back to the start in two minutes. Just before going again, he records his heart rate

3. repeats 1 and 2 five more times

4. after the 6th repetition he takes his heart rate again

5. while recovering he records his heart rate every minute for 10 minutes.

Jack's partner asks him to rate his effort on a scale of 6 to 20. A score of 6 means he did not try. A score of 20 is his maximum effort. Jack's partner then trains and Jack records his results.

Both athletes perform a suitable cool-down.

Session B: Tom's training for a 1500m run

Tom, like his brother, works with a partner, so they can record each other's results.
Before starting the warm-up Tom and his partner record their heart rates while at rest. Sometimes they also take their blood pressure.
After warming up appropriately, Tom begins his interval training session from a standing start on a 400m (or 200m) track.
He then:

1. runs for three minutes at a good pace, about 75 per cent effort – his partner records his heart rate and notes the distance he ran

2. walks back slowly to the start to allow three minutes recovery time. His heart rate is once more recorded before he runs again

3. repeats 1 and 2 a further four times

4. after the fourth repetition, his heart rate is recorded again

5. while recovering, Tom records his heart rate every minute for 10 minutes.

Tom's partner then asks him to rate his effort on a scale of 6 to 20. A score of 6 means he did not try. A score of 20 is his maximum effort.

Tom's partner then completes the same session and Tom records his heart rates.

Both athletes then perform a cool-down. To finish the session they record each other's heart rate, and possibly each other's blood pressure.

Points to learn from this exercise

◉ Session A is short distance work. From a rolling start, the athletes will run at a very fast pace thereby improving their speed (SRF) (principle of specificity) as well as their cardiovascular fitness.

◉ Each of these sessions uses the principle of **specificity** matching the method of training to the aspect of each activity which is to be improved.

◉ The heart rate taken at the end of each repetition is called the **working heart rate**.

◉ This type of training includes periods of work followed by periods of rest, therefore it is interval training.

In session A the rest allows the athlete to recover, pay back the oxygen debt and disperse the build up of lactic acid in the muscles. The work done can therefore be of high intensity, the I for intensity in the FITT principle. Session B, although it is interval training, is of lower intensity and helps to build up the athlete's cardiovascular fitness. The ability to work the whole body for long periods of time still helps athletes to improve their speed.

Apply it!

Try these two training sessions in different lessons and feel the difference. Each member of the group will need a heart rate monitor and a training partner to help to monitor their heart rates. Take and record your heart rate while at rest before starting to warm up. You could also take your blood pressure before you start and again after you finish.

You could perform these sessions on a weekly basis as part of your personal exercise programme.

Task 1
work out from the chart how many minutes it took for Tom's working heart rate to return to the resting heart rate.

Plot your heart rate on a chart like this after performing these exercise sessions.

Task 2
In your group discuss the following questions:
1. What aspect of fitness were you training for, health-related exercise or skill-related fitness?
2. Which part of either health-related exercise or skill-related fitness were you training for?
3. Was your heart rate higher in session A or B?
4. In which session were you most out of breath?

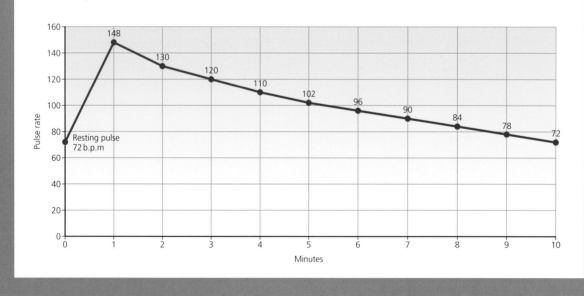

Tom's recovery rate after the exercise session

edexcel ⫶⫶⫶ examiner tip

If you are asked in an exam which athlete uses speed the most, give the most obvious answer: in this case, the answer would be Jack, the 100 metres sprinter.

Aerobic and anaerobic fitness

Both of these sessions would improve cardiovascular fitness, but in different ways.

● Session A is anaerobic, meaning without air. Performers would be out of breath after the exercise, because the body has been working at a very high intensity. Athletes also breathe heavier after anaerobic exercise because the body, which requires extra oxygen when working, has not been provided with enough oxygen during the exercise. The 100m sprint is an anaerobic event so this form of training is suitable. This session is also designed to focus on improving speed over a short distance, which is essential for a 100 metres runner.

● Session B is more suited to aerobic fitness, meaning with air, because it is of a lower intensity and performers would breathe continuously throughout it. This is why performers get less breathless in this session. This session improves speed to the level needed for a 1500m runner.

These sessions are similar in that they are both interval training (a period of work followed by a period of rest), but they develop different types of cardiovascular fitness.

Print a copy of your recovery rates for both of your training sessions.

Did your heart rate recover to your resting heart rate within the 10 minutes recovery time for either session A or session B?

Which session did you recover from most quickly?

edexcel ⠿ key terms

Aerobic: 'With oxygen'. If exercise is not too fast and is steady, the heart can supply all the oxygen muscles need.

Anaerobic: 'Without oxygen'. If exercise is done in short, fast bursts, the heart cannot supply blood and oxygen to muscles as fast as the cells use them.

ResultsPlus
Build Better Answers

The following are methods of training:

A   Weight training

B   Sprint training

C   Cross training

D   Continuous training

To answer questions (a)–(c), select one of the letters A, B, C, or D for the correct method of training.

(a) Ade runs in the school cross country team and competes in the shot putt event at his local club. Which training method should Ade use to improve his performance in the shot?

(b) Which training method should Ade use to improve his time in the cross country?

(c) Which training method would allow Ade to combine the training needs of both of his events?

(Total 3 marks)

TS answer: (a) A, (b) D, (c) C

Examiner comment: Sprint training is not a method of training. If you know this you only have three options. To apply your knowledge in C, it is essential that you know that cross training is a combination of training methods.

LINK IT UP!

To learn more about breathing during exercise see CH 28. If you want to remind yourself about cardiovascular fitness go to CH 8.

16: Analysing training sessions

Objectives

By the end of this chapter you should:

○ understand what is meant by resting heart rate, working heart rate, and recovery rate, and be able to evaluate results on a graph

○ be able to use graphs to demonstrate and explain the use of target zones and the thresholds of training.

Analysing training is essential to monitoring ability and improvements. Without analysis it would be impossible to know whether the sessions were having an effect.

To analyse a training session properly, it is necessary to know what to record and what the results can show.

edexcel ▦ examiner tip

When answering a question on heart rate, remember that heart rate is the number of times the heart beats per minute, not the number of times the heart beats. Candidates lose marks for not adding the two words: per minute.

Heart rate is the number of times that the heart beats per minute (BPM).

Resting heart rate is the heart rate at rest. It is best taken first thing in the morning before getting out of bed. It is normally between 60 to 80 beats per minute. A person who exercises regularly may have a resting heart rate of 50 to 60 beats per minute, whereas an athlete in full-time training could have a resting heart rate of between 40 and 50, or even lower. One of the effects of regular exercise and training is a lower resting heart rate, so this is a very good measure of fitness. A lower heart rate means that the heart is more efficient as it pumps the same amount of blood around the body with fewer beats. In other words, the heart has to beat less often, so is less stressed.

Measuring heart rate can be done by checking the radial pulse. This is done by putting the index and middle fingers on the palm side of the wrist just below the thumb. However, the most accurate way is to wear a heart rate monitor.

Working heart rate is the measurement of the heart rate during or immediately after exercise. This is an accurate guide to the intensity (the I in the FITT principle) of the exercise or how hard the heart is working. The higher the working heart rate, the harder it is working.

Apply it!

If you had a normal heart rate of 72 beats per minute work out how many times your heart would beat in an hour. Now work out how many times your heart would beat in an hour if you had a resting heart rate of 56 beats per minute.
Work out the total difference in the number of beats in a day.

Maximum heart rate (MHR) is calculated according to a person's age. Maximum heart rate can be calculated by subtracting the person's age from 220. The figure 220 is taken as the maximum heart rate of a new-born baby.
220 – age = maximum heart rate (BPM).

This is the same for men and for women, so for a 16-year-old, maximum heart rate is
220 – 16 = 204 BPM.

Target heart rate or target zone can be found by taking 60 per cent of MHR as the lower threshold and 80 per cent as the upper threshold. If the MHR is 204, the lower threshold will be 122.4 and the upper will be 163.2. The aim when training is to be within this target zone, which means that the person is working at a worthwhile level of training (working harder than usual) and will get fitter. Many people, both athletes and people who train simply to be fit, can use this as a guideline, although athletes may well train with their heart rates above this level and will certainly have their heart rates above this level when competing often for a prolonged period of time.

Recovery rate is the measure of how long it takes for a person's heart rate to return to its resting level after a training session. The sooner the heart rate returns to normal, the fitter the person is. As the resting heart rate is a good measure of a person's fitness level, a quicker recovery heart rate also suggests a higher fitness level. It is useful to know resting and recovery rates as they are a guide to fitness level and a yardstick by which any increase or decrease in fitness can be measured.

Apply it!

1. How long did it take for the person's highest working heart rate to recover to the resting heart rate?

2. If this person is 16, what method of training would you expect them to be using to produce these results.

3. After the person reaches their highest heart rate, how many minutes does it take for their heart rate to come out of the target zone.

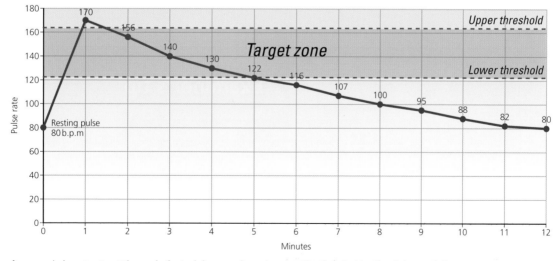

A person's heart rate at the end of a training session, showing the thresholds of training and the target zone.

examzone

Know Zone
Topic 1.1.4: Physical activity as part of your healthy, active lifestyle

This is another big topic with lots to learn on a wide variety of subjects from testing to training, and principles of training, to graphical analysis of training performance. You need to be able to apply this knowledge and give examples.

You should know...

- ☐ What is meant by a PAR-Q.
- ☐ How to assess health-related exercise, and skill-related fitness using a number of tests.
- ☐ How to explain the principles of training – individual needs / differences, progressive overload, specificity, rest and recovery, the FITT principle, and reversibility.
- ☐ How to use these principles to improve your fitness and/or skills in a personal exercise programme.
  - How components overlap with other principles of training.
  - How application of the FITT principle can improve performance and competence.
- ☐ The term 'reversibility'.
- ☐ How to describe and explain the principles of setting SMART targets.
- ☐ How to apply SMART goals (specific, measurable, achievable, realistic, time-bound) when setting up a personal exercise programme in order to gain maximum benefit from it.

- ☐ The six different training methods: interval, continuous, fartlek, circuit, weight, and cross.
  - Which sports and activities each is most suited to.
  - How each can improve health and fitness.
  - Their relationships with the components of fitness.
- ☐ How to explain a warm-up, main activity and cool-down and the importance of each in connection with a training session.
- ☐ How methods of training can be used to create different effects and improve physical performance and how they can be used to match individual needs and differences.
- ☐ What is meant by resting heart rate, working heart rate, and recovery rate, and be able to evaluate results on a graph.
- ☐ How to use graphs to demonstrate and explain the use of target zones and the thresholds of training.

Key terms

Physical activity
PAR-Q
PEP
Progressive overload
Individual needs/differences
FITT
Specificity
Rest
Recovery
Reversibility
SMART
Methods of training
Aerobic
Anaerobic
Target zone
Training thresholds

Examiner's tip

You must know and use the principles of training in the specification (and listed above). Think about how you used them in your PEP. Read your PEP the night before the theory paper examination to remind yourself of how you used them and the other points in this topic such as the training methods.

Question: The principles of training should be applied to make sure your training is effective. Complete the table below by naming and explaining four principles of training which you applied in your personal exercise programme (PEP). You are not allowed to use the FITT principle as one of your principles of training to answer this question.

Students' answer

Principle of training	Explanation of principle
(i) Interval	Do an activity, have a break, then do it again
(ii) Circuit	Do different exercises in a circuit
(iii) Fartlek	Run a distance, jog a distance, then walk
(iv) Weight	Do a normal activity but use weights when you are doing it

Examiners' comments

◼ Poor 0/8. This candidate has scored no points on this question because he has completely mixed up the principles of training with the methods of training. Dropping 8 marks like this could cost a grade C pass. You must read the question closely. Only 20% of the candidates scored 2/2 for i. 25% scored 2/2 for ii and iii. 18% scored 2/2 for iv. Overall students struggled to name a principle of training then explain it.

Build Better Answers

Individual Needs – I planned my programme for what I wanted to improve

Specificity – I matched my training to what I wanted to improve

Progressive overload – I gradually made my training harder as I got fitter

Reversibility – I had an injury and could not train for two weeks so I lost some fitness during that time

Know the principles of training and in this case if you used them in your PEP you could just explain how you used them for 8 marks. Remember to read your PEP the night before your theory examination. It will remind you of what you did and you may be requested to apply your knowledge as in this question.

Practice Exam Questions

John has planned to do circuit training as part of his personal exercise programme to improve his general fitness. He has chosen to do press ups as one of the exercises.

A What two components of fitness might he be trying to improve through this exercise? (2)

B State three other exercises John could include to improve his general fitness. (3)

C Why is it important to consider the order of the exercises when planning his circuit? (1)

D John wants to improve his cardiovascular fitness and he knows that to do this he must exercise with his heart rate in the target zone. Explain what is meant by the target zone. (1)

E If John is 16 years old explain how you would calculate his target zone. (1)

F When John does his circuit some of the exercises produce short quick movements and he gets quite breathless. What is the name given to this type of exercise? (1)

G If John continues to exercise regularly over a long period of time what is likely to happen to his resting heart rate? (1)

Topic 1.1.5: Your personal health and wellbeing

Sport in Context

Without a balanced lifestyle your personal health and wellbeing will suffer. If you have a healthy diet and do regular workouts you are likely to feel better and be healthier. Athletes such as Iwan Thomas, a former Olympic runner, and Phillips Idowu, an Olympic triple jumper, follow a strict diet and prepare for an event by eating exactly what their bodies need so they can perform at their best.

In this topic you will learn the importance of balancing exercise, diet, work and rest. You will learn about a balanced diet and how to plan your training so that you build up your fitness while allowing enough rest to rebuild damaged tissue and give your body time to recover before the next exercise session.

PE and me

1. How would you describe a balanced lifestyle?

2. Do you think you have a balanced lifestyle?

3. Would you describe your diet as healthy? Why?

4. Why would a 400m runner and a triple-jumper have different diets?

5. What would you eat before a game?

Topic Overview

By the end of this topic you should:

◉ understand the link between diet, exercise, work and rest

◉ be able to explain the importance of a balanced diet

◉ understand how the timing of food intake before performing needs to be considered.

17: The link between exercise, diet, work and rest

Objectives

By the end of these pages you should be able to:

- understand the links between exercise, diet, work and rest and how these factors influence your personal health and wellbeing
- explain the requirements of a balanced diet
- recall the factors of a balanced diet
- explain how each of these factors fits into a balanced, healthy lifestyle.

Apply it!

Do you know anyone who is on a special diet?

If so, is this for medical, religious, moral or health reasons e.g. food allergy?

Give an example of what they can eat. What can't they eat?

Exercise, diet, work and rest

It is important to understand the connections between exercise, diet, work and rest. Each has an equal part to play in ensuring happiness and wellbeing. Work can provide finance, motivation and opportunity, and exercise the fitness necessary to work and enjoy life. Adequate rest maintains a balance between the two. Perhaps this is best summed up by the proverb 'all work and no play make Jack a dull boy'. Finally, a balanced diet provides all the essential nutrients for health, fitness, strength and wellbeing.

The importance of a balanced diet

The word 'diet' is sometimes misunderstood. Diet can be defined as 'the normal food we eat' but there are also special diets, such as vegan, vegetarian, gluten free, and so on. People may adopt a special diet to control their body composition or body weight, but they may also follow a special diet for moral or religious reasons, or because they have an allergy to certain types of food, e.g. the gluten in wheat, or dairy products.

Diet is an essential part of providing the energy needed to work and exercise, and also to rest and repair tissues. The energy balance must be considered: calories in should equal calories out – in other words, the number of calories in the diet should be the same as the number of calories used.

Active people use more energy so they need more calories in their diet and more of the foods that provide them. A balanced diet is not just about calories and energy, it is about providing the body with all the nutrients it requires to work as effectively as possible. A balanced diet includes seven factors, and these will now be explained.

The factors of a balanced diet

You need to understand the seven factors that contribute to a balanced diet as they each provide something different for a balanced, healthy lifestyle. For example, carbohydrates provide energy while protein builds muscle; both are very important for everybody, and especially for active people who exercise and play sport regularly. The diagram below may help you to remember and apply these factors, or you could make up your own acronym.

Macro nutrients

Carbohydrates are important because they give us energy. There are two types of carbohydrate, complex and simple.

- Complex carbohydrates are often referred to as starch, and are found in natural foods such as bananas, brown rice, wholemeal bread, wholemeal pasta, nuts, and potatoes. Foods of this type these help provide energy to exercise and should form about 50 per cent of our daily intake.

- Simple carbohydrates are also known as sugars. In their natural form, they are found in fruit and vegetables. Refined sugars are found in biscuits, cakes, chocolate, and confectionary.

Carbohydrates are stored in the muscles and the liver as glycogen, which is quickly converted into glucose and used to provide energy.

The energy needed to work and exercise should come from complex carbohydrates because they provide a slower and longer-lasting release of energy than simple carbohydrates, and can contribute to good long-term health.

Fats are important because they provide energy and, together with glycogen, help muscles to work. Fats are found in butter, margarine and cooking oils. They can also be found in foods such as bacon, cheese, oily fish and nuts.

The daily intake of fats to provide energy should be about 30 per cent of the total diet.

Protein is important to help build muscles and to repair damaged tissue. Protein is also used to provide energy during extended periods of exercise, such as marathon running, when all the carbohydrate has been used up.

Protein comes from two types of food: two-thirds is found in animal protein, and one-third in plant or vegetable protein.

- Animal protein is found in meat, poultry, fish, and dairy products such as milk, cheese and yoghurt. Eggs are also a good source of protein.

- Plant or vegetable protein is found in pulses (lentils, peas and beans), nuts, bread, potatoes, breakfast cereal, pasta, and rice. Some of these foods are also a source of carbohydrate.

People who follow a vegan diet eat no animal products and so have to get their protein from cereals, nuts, and pulses.

Protein is important to a balanced, healthy lifestyle because without it it would not be possible to build muscle and repair injuries to muscles, which would make physical activity very hard!

ResultsPlus
Build Better Answers

Weight loss as a result of physical activity is achieved by… (2 marks)

Correct answer is: 1st mark for reference to 'more/ working harder' than you normally do

2nd mark for reference to 'using more calories than taken in' (or equivalent)

Examiner: energy balance is an important topic you need to understand because it involves both diet and exercise.

Micro nutrients

Minerals are essential for a healthy body. They include:

- **Calcium** is vital to health, especially during growth in childhood and adolescence. It is important in the formation of bones and teeth, and helps to make the bones strong. Bones reach their peak mass, or at their strongest, when people are around 30 to 35 years of age; after this age there is a gradual decrease. It is important to maintain calcium intake as people get older so as to reduce the likelihood of osteoporosis, a condition which causes bones to become thin and weak. Milk, cheese and cereals are the main source of calcium in the diet.

Calcium is important to a balanced, healthy lifestyle because strong bones are necessary in order to withstand the impact of exercise and of everyday life.

- **Iron** is essential to the blood because of its links with haemoglobin and its effect on the oxygen carrying capacity of the blood and the formation of red blood cells. Iron is therefore very important to a healthy, balanced lifestyle as without it, it would not be possible to for the blood to carry oxygen around the body. Lack of iron can lead to a condition called anaemia which causes tiredness, lethargy, shortness of breath and palpitations (irregular heart beat). Many foods contain iron but iron in meat is absorbed more easily.

LINK IT UP!

For more information about the body types go to CH 19.

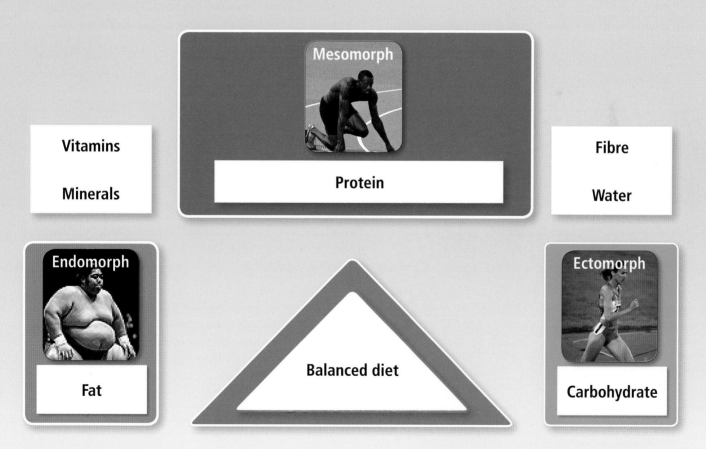

Each of the 3 macro nutrients are required in different body shapes, somatotypes. Endomorphs have more fat (e.g. sumo wrestlers) mesomorphs need more protein (e.g. sprinters) and ectomorphs need more carbohydrates to allow them to run further and faster (e.g. marathon runners). Everybody needs the micro nutrients and minerals, and fibre and water.

Other minerals

- Sodium is needed for regulating body water content and is also involved with nerve functioning.

- Potassium is important to the functioning of cells.

- Trace elements such as zinc and selenium are needed in very small amounts.

Vitamins are essential to health. Among other things, vitamins are necessary for:

- good vision

- good skin

- red blood cell formation

- healing

- healthy bones and teeth

- blood clotting.

Vitamins come in two groups; water soluble (vitamins that can be dissolved in water e.g. B and C) and fat soluble (those that can be dissolved in fat e.g. A, D and E) – which is one of the reasons fat is needed in the diet.

- Vitamin A is found in milk, cheese, egg yolk, liver and carrots. It is necessary for vision and helps to prevent night blindness.

- Vitamin B1 is needed to release carbohydrate, and is found in whole grains, nuts and meat.

- Vitamin C is found in fruit and vegetables. It helps healing and fighting infection and the maintenance of bones, teeth, and gums.

- Vitamin D is found in milk, fish, liver and eggs. Sunshine is also a good source of Vitamin D. It is needed for the absorption of calcium, which is necessary for healthy bones.

- Vitamin E is found in vegetable oil, wholemeal bread and cereals, and is needed for growth and development.

A balanced supply of vitamins is essential for the body to function properly, and therefore important to a balanced healthy lifestyle.

> **edexcel ⋮⋮⋮ examiner tip**
>
> Make sure you know and can explain how the minerals calcium and iron are needed and used, and why.

Water

Water accounts for around half of body weight. It holds oxygen and is the main component of many cells. It transports nutrients, waste and hormones around the body and controls the distribution of electrolytes (or body salts). During exercise, the body sweats and loses electrolytes. Some isotonic drinks claim to replace these, but a balanced diet will also do this naturally.

So why is water so important in physical activity and sport, and for a balanced healthy lifestyle? Water is essential to control temperature, especially when exercising and playing sport, and drinking at least eight glasses a day is often recommended.

Most athletes and sportspeople need liquid when competing in order to improve their performance and to offset dehydration. Boxers and jockeys often make themselves sweat to lose weight so that they can reach the required weight for competition, but this may make them vulnerable to dehydration.

84

Fibre

Fibre adds bulk to food and aids the functioning of the digestive system. Fibre (roughage) is found in the leaves, stems, roots, seeds and fruits of plants. The fibre content of some foods may be reduced when they are processed and peeled.

There are two types of fibre: soluble and insoluble. It is important to eat a variety of food to so that both types are included. Wholegrain cereal and wholegrain bread are sources of insoluble fibre, which is required as a bulking agent and to prevent constipation. Oats, fruit and vegetables are sources of soluble fibre which helps to reduce blood cholesterol levels.

Fibre is important to a healthy, active lifestyle because the digestive system does not operate properly without it. The body would not be able to get rid of waste products, which would lead to many diseases.

Wellbeing

Diet makes an important and valuable contribution to wellbeing and ability to function. A balanced diet provides all the nutrients needed to exercise and work. Appropriate rest periods are necessary to allow the body to repair and grow using the nutrients provided by diet.

Apply it!

1. Read the label on a pack of butter or tub of spread for information on fats. Note the name of the product, the total fat content, and how it is broken down into saturated, polyunsaturated, and monounsaturated fats. Note also the total energy, which may be shown in both kilojoules and kilo calories. The energy should be shown per 100 grams.

2. Have a good look at your breakfast cereal packet. Write down the names of the vitamins contained in the cereal and make a note of what they are needed for.

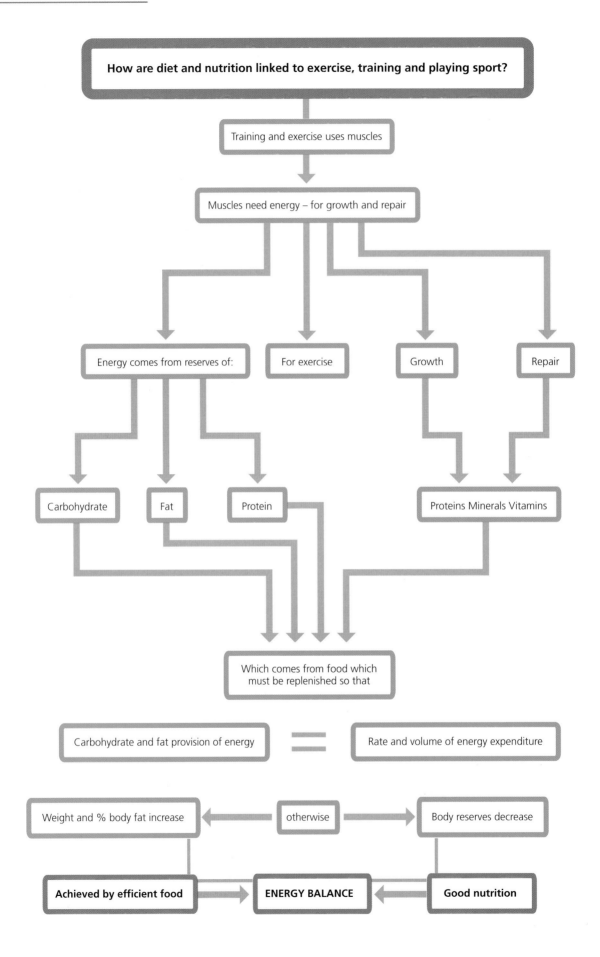

ResultsPlus
Exam Question Report

Fibre, vitamins and minerals are important parts of a balanced diet. Complete the table below by:

(i) Naming four other nutritional requirements of a balanced diet.

(ii) Explaining how each helps to participate in sport
(8 marks, June 2006)

Answers to part i and ii

	(i) Nutritional requirement	**(ii) How this helps participate in sport**
1	Carbohydrates	Provides energy
2	Fats	Provides energy
3	Proteins	Growth and repair, therefore repairs damaged tissue (or equivalent); increase in muscle size (or equivalent)
4	Water	Prevents dehydration/ replaces water lost through exercise

How students answered part i

Some candidates put calcium which is not one of the seven factors in its own right, but is part of the group of minerals. Minerals have already been mentioned in the question, which asks for four other factors. Try not to make these two simple mistakes: putting an answer which is part of one of the factors, but not one in its own right, or by not reading the question.

15% 0–1 marks

This is not a hard question - all candidates should aim to know the factors of a balanced diet and be able to recall them.

42% 2–3 marks

Most candidates (43%) got all four correct which gives them a much better chance of scoring good marks on the explanation part of the question.

43% 4 marks

How students answered part ii

Many candidates lost marks on part ii because part i was wrong.

36% 0–1 marks

The explanations to these questions are not difficult, for example, carbohydrate and fat provide energy to play, and protein helps to build and repair muscle, while water prevents dehydration.

47% 2–3 marks

Some students (17%) did well, by giving simple accurate answers and getting part (i) of the question right.

17% 4 marks

18: Dietary intake and performance

Objectives

By the end of this chapter you should be able to:

- explain the importance of the right timing of dietary intake for optimum performance
- understand and explain blood flow (blood shunting) during exercise.

The timing of dietary intake for optimum performance

The factors of a balanced diet play an important part in leading a healthy, active lifestyle, preparing for physical activity, and taking part in sport. It is also important to consider not only what to eat for best performance, but when to eat it.

Carbo-loading

The energy to run comes from food, and running does not get much harder than the London Marathon. So what should the runners eat, and how should they prepare their diet before the race? From what we have learned so far, we know that carbohydrates will be the main source of fuel for the runners and that there is a plan which they can follow which will help them to prepare for the race.

Carbo-loading refers to a system used mostly by marathon runners, and also by other athletes who take part in ultra-distance events such as triathlons. It is designed to make maximum use of the athlete's energy resources and your knowledge of the nutrients of a balanced diet will help you to understand how it works.

Suppose members of your local running club have entered the London Marathon and are completing their final training. It's Sunday, a week before the marathon. Today they will go for a very long run of at least 20 miles, with over two hours of running. What will this do to their energy stores? Your answer should be that it will deplete them, run them down very low.

Over the next few days their training programme will reduce in frequency and distance but be of a higher quality as they rest and recover and taper towards the race (this is the intensity principle that we looked at in CH 11). However, their diet will be low in carbohydrate, but high in protein rich foods (meat, fish, dairy products, eggs and pulses). You should know from what you've learnt so far that on this diet their energy stores will remain low, since protein supplies the body with much less energy than carbohydrates.

However, on Wednesday the club members will change their diet to include very high levels of carbohydrate so as to fill their energy stores completely in preparation for the race on Sunday. Their training will be over shorter distances but at a much faster pace, sharpening up their speed for the race. On the Friday and Saturday before the race they will take part in one of the London Marathon's famous 'pasta parties'. And what nutrient does pasta contain? Carbohydrate!

In this way the runners' body systems will be fooled into retaining excessive amounts of carbohydrate, because they were starved of it in the early part of the week. This gives them a greater energy store to draw on during the race itself.

Tuesday

Wednesday

This example shows how knowing what nutrients are needed, why, and when, can help a particular sport get maximum results. In the early part of the week, eating more protein will help the runners' muscles to repair after higher intensity sessions. Later in the week, eating high levels of carbohydrates will help the runners to pack in and store as much carbohydrate as possible, which will in turn increase the glycogen stores in the liver and the muscles, ready for use in the race itself.

It is also important to take food in the first two hours after a race, sporting event, or training session as it is necessary to restock on carbohydrates used up during the activity. Isotonic drinks have a similar carbohydrate electrolyte concentration to the body's own fluids and can be used in the recovery process to boost energy intake.

Blood flow during exercise
At the beginning of exercise, blood is sent to the working muscle. Less blood is therefore available to digest food in the gut, which can cause cramps and stomach discomfort. This flow of blood from other areas into the muscle is known as blood shunting. This is why an exercise session should not start until at least 2–3 hours after the last meal.

examzone
Know Zone
Topic 1.1.5: Your personal health and wellbeing

This topic will help you to understand how exercise, diet, work and rest come together and how they can give you a balance in your personal health and wellbeing.

You should know...

- [ ] The links between exercise, diet, work and rest and how these factors influence your personal health and wellbeing.
- [ ] The requirements of a balanced diet.
- [ ] Recall the factors of a balanced diet.
- [ ] How each of these factors fits into a balanced, healthy lifestyle.
- [ ] The importance of the right timing of dietary intake for optimum performance.
- [ ] About blood flow (blood shunting) during exercise.

Key terms

Exercise, diet, work and rest
Balanced diet
- Macro nutrients
- Carbohydrate
- Protein
- Fat

- Micro nutrients
- Water
- Vitamins
- Fibre
- Minerals

Stretch activity

You have learned a lot about exercise. You have planned and may already have performed your personal exercise programme (PEP). Your PEP will have to fit in with your work, and you should understand the importance of a balanced diet and fitting in the principles of training, rest and recovery so that you can recover from exercise and your body has time to adapt.

Support activity

Fit exercise around your work commitments and allow time for recovery. If you are exercising more consider what and when you eat. Will you need more carbohydrate and/or protein? Will you need to drink more water? Will you use energy drinks? How will they help you? Read the labels. Andy Murray's fitness coach Jez Green says 'train hard, train SMART and recover well'.

Examiner's tip

Remember the parts of a balanced diet.
Be able to apply your knowledge:
e.g. energy = carbohydrate and fat; muscle building and repair = protein; water = to avoid dehydration.

ResultsPlus
Maximise your marks

Question: Jack plays rugby at school and for a local club. He has been told by his club that he should be more careful about the food he eats, so that he has the necessary energy to participate and is not carrying any unnecessary weight. Fibre, vitamins and minerals are important parts of a balanced diet.

Complete the table below by:
▲ (i) naming three other nutritional requirements of a balanced diet

⚪ (ii) explaining how each helps Jack to participate in sport.

	(i) Nutritional Requirement	(ii) How this helps Jack participate in sport
1		
2		
3		

3 marks for each correct nutritional requirement and 3 marks for each explanation of how it helps Jack to participate in sport. (6 marks)

	Students' answer	Examiners' comments	Build Better Answers
1	(i) Protein (ii) Repairs broken muscles	(i) Correct answer (ii) This candidate was given the benefit of the doubt but you should try to be accurate – you don't break a muscle!	Growth and repair or increase muscle size
2	(i) Carbohydrates (ii) Gives energy	(i) Correct answer (ii) This candidate would have been given a mark, as the answer was almost right.	Provides energy
3	(i) Calcium (ii)	(i) This is a wrong answer; the student has used a specific mineral and mineral is one of the non-acceptable answers mentioned in the question. Because the first part of the question is wrong then the second part is also going to be wrong. This is not thought of as being a difficult question so you need to score well on this topic.	Fat Fat provides energy

Examiner's comment

For a question that is generally not considered to be difficult, on the whole a very small proportion of students gained full marks. Fewer than 50% gave four of the factors of a balanced diet, even fever few able to give correct explanations. Also, if students get the first part wrong the second part cannot be correct as they are explaining the wrong thing.

Practice Exam Questions

1 Which of the following is a source of roughage in an athlete's diet? (1)

A Fats

B Vitamins

C Minerals

D Fibre

2 Which of the following gives a balanced diet to maintain body requirements when undertaking an exercise programme? (1)

A Carbohydrate, fibre, vitamins, minerals, water, protein

B Water, carbohydrates, protein

C Fats, carbohydrates, fibre, vitamins, minerals, water, protein

D Carbohydrates, proteins, water, vitamins, minerals

Topic 1.2.1: Physical activity and your healthy mind and body

Sport in Context

Whatever their shape, most people can take part in physical activity. Look at the runners in the London Marathon, and you will see people of all shapes and sizes, all taking part for their own reasons. In this topic you will learn about body shape and why particular sports tend to be associated with certain body shapes, or somatotypes. You will learn about optimum weight, how it varies and how it can affect involvement in exercise and physical activity.

This topic will help you to understand more about the effects of drugs – including nicotine, alcohol and performance-enhancing drugs – on health and wellbeing. You will learn how to identify risks, how to prepare for exercise using a PAR-Q and the correct equipment, and how to follow the rules of participation.

PE and me

1. What kinds of body type do you think there are?

2. What sports do you think your body type is best suited to? Why?

3. Do you think it is very important to be a certain shape to succeed in a sport?

4. Can you describe anorexia and obesity?

Topic Overview

By the end of this topic you will be able to:

- describe the different body types (somatotypes) and the typical sports with which they are associated
- explain optimum weight and how it varies, and the meaning of a number of terms related to weight, including anorexia and obesity
- describe how to prevent injury and reduce risk.

19: Different body types

Objectives

By the end of this chapter you will be able to:

- describe the different body types (somatotypes): endomorph, mesomorph, ectomorph
- explain the effect each can have on participation and performance
- identify activities where different body types are an advantage.

Somatotype

Bodies come in all shapes and sizes but can be grouped into three basic types, called somatotypes:

- endomorph
- mesomorph
- ectomorph.

An important factor in performance is body build or physique. This can be measured to give a person's somatotype.

Somatotype refers to three characteristics of a person's body:

1. fatness (endomorphy)
2. muscularity (mesomorphy)
3. linearity, or thinness and height in relation to weight (ectomorphy).

Each of these factors, when measured, is graded out of seven.

For example, an athlete's somatotype might be 2:6:3, which means 2/7 for fatness, 6/7 for muscle, and 3/7 for thinness.
Most people's bodies are a mixture of all three types. Extreme examples of sportspeople's body types might be:

- endomorph – sumo wrestler
- mesomorph – 100m sprinter
- ectomorph – long-distance runner.

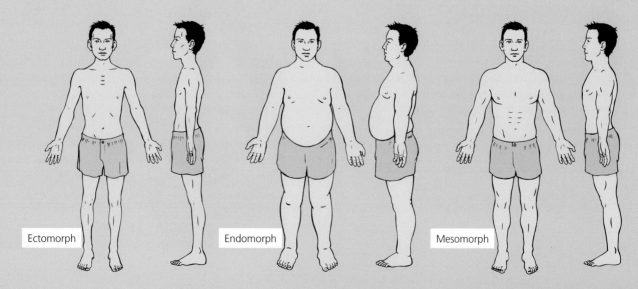

Ectomorph   Endomorph   Mesomorph

Finding your somatotype

Height, weight, bone size, and muscle girth measurements as well as fat content are used to find a person's somatotype. Once all these measurements have been taken, the somatotype can be found by using a computer programme or a chart.

It is difficult to measure young people's somatotypes as they may be growing rapidly. The charts are designed for younger children and adults as little change in physique will occur at these times.

How to measure your somatotype

You need to record a number of measurements:

- Record your height and weight.
- To take a measurement of bone size you will need a condyle calliper. Using this, measure the widest point across the elbow, and then the knee.
- Muscle girth can be recorded by measuring round the widest part of the biceps and gastrocnemius muscles.
- To measure fat content, skinfold measurements are taken at three sites: the triceps and the subscapula and the suprailiac. Take a fold of skin between the thumb and forefinger, then put the calliper over it and record the result in millimetres.

Once measurements are taken, the results are entered into a table to get our somatotype. Once you have worked out your somatotype, you can plot it on to a somato chart.

Apply it!

If you have plotted your own somatotype on a chart, exchange scores with other students and plot their scores on your chart.

Somatotypes in sport

Certain body types are more suited to certain sports. To take athletics as an example, it is not surprising that throwers (who are predominantly mesomorphic endomorphs) tend to be a different shape to high jumpers (who are predominantly ectomorphic mesomorphs). An analysis of somato charts reveals that athletes from certain sports tend to be grouped together.

- **Endomorphs** are often grouped in sports that depend on power, for example forwards in rugby. Their extra body fat means that they can literally get more weight behind themselves, or their actions.

- **Mesomorphs** tend to be involved in sports which require strength and sudden bursts of energy, rather than sustained effort over long distances. Their muscular build often means they are stronger and better able to cope with anaerobic exercise.

- **Ectomorphs** tend to excel at long distance events, such as the marathon.

So what is a mesomorphic endomorph or an ectomorphic mesomorph? These terms are used to describe body types which fall between the three basic types.

Take throwers, who are predominantly endomorphic mesomorphs. This means their highest rating is in mesomorphy (muscle), and their second highest rating is in endomorphy (fat). The high jumpers who are predominantly mesomorphic ectomorphs would have their highest rating in ectomorphy (linearity/thinness) and their second highest rating in mesomorphy (muscle). These examples show that the optimum body type is often a mixture of two somatotypes, for example combining muscle and fat or linearity and muscle.

Apply it!

If you have plotted your class somatotype results, can you spot any trends?

edexcel key terms

Somatotype: classification of body type

endomorph: an individual with wide hips and narrow shoulders, characterised by fatness

mesomorph: an individual with wide shoulders and narrow hips, characterised by muscularity

ectomorph: an individual with narrow shoulders and narrow hips, characterised by thinness.

ResultsPlus
Exam Question Report

Complete the statements below about different body types.
(a) _____ tend to be very muscular.
(b) Ectomorphs have a very slim build, they tend to be tall and _____ . Ectomorphs have a suitable body type for _____ (2) (June 2008, 3 marks)

Answers

(a) Mesomorph/s, Mesomorphic. Metamorph would not be acceptable

(b) Blank 1: Thin/lean/skinny/equivalent. Unacceptable answers were: slim, light, wiry, gangly, under weight (as in question)

Blank 2: Aerobic/endurance/1500m or greater/High Jump/jockeys equivalent. Unacceptable answers were: Basketball players/gymnasts

How Students answered (a)

Three quarters of students got this question correct. You must get this type of question correct if you are to do well.

25%	0 marks
75%	2 marks

How Students answered (b)

Apart from some minor confusion this question was well answered. The most common error was where candidates repeated the question word 'slim' when completing blank 1. You must know the somatotypes and be able to define them if needed in the exam paper.

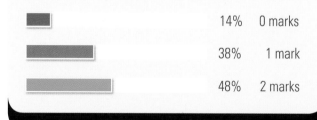

14%	0 marks
38%	1 mark
48%	2 marks

20: Optimum weight

Objectives

By the end of this chapter you will understand:

- optimum weight and why it varies according to height, gender, bone structure and muscle girth
- how optimum weight can affect performance and participation in physical activity.

Optimum weight

The dictionary definition of 'optimum' is 'most favourable' or 'best compromise' (*Oxford English Dictionary*). A person's favourable optimum weight could be with reference to general lifestyle or a specific sport. Most sportspeople get to know the weight at which they perform best and make sure that they stay as near to it as they can. Other people can find their optimum weight by using the BMI index. They can also find it by measuring wrist girth.

Factors affecting optimum weight

Height: taller people are usually, although not always, heavier than shorter people.

Gender: men and women have different body composition; men tend to have more muscle and larger bones. Therefore males and females have different charts to find their optimum weight.

Bone structure: bodies have different bone structures, sometimes referred to as frame size. For instance, two men of the same height may have completely different bone structures: one could have broad shoulders and thick wrists, the other narrow shoulders and hips, and thin wrists. The man with the larger frame would not have a similar optimum weight to the man with narrow shoulders and hips, primarily because the bones in his body would weigh much more.

Muscle girth: as with bone structure, people naturally have different muscle girth which means that they weigh more; simple charts that measure optimum weight only according to height may suggest that these people are overweight. In most cases, muscle girth increases with training. Therefore sportspeople who need strong muscles, such as England rugby star Andrew Sheridan, have a large muscle girth.

Genetics: body weight and shape are largely passed on through the genes from parent to child.

Body composition is defined as the percentage of body weight that is fat, muscle and bone so all three of these factors affect a person's weight.

Optimum weight in sport

The optimum weight for individual sportspeople varies widely according to the sport; rugby and horseracing, for example, have quite different requirements. In rugby, a forward's job is to use muscular strength and power to push in the scrum and tackle in defence. Therefore, optimum weight may be high compared with people of similar height as forwards need a lot of muscular strength, which comes as a result of large muscle girth. On the other hand, a jockey needs to be short in height, with small bone structure and a minimum amount of muscle. These factors result in a low weight, which is optimum in this case as it allows the horse to gallop faster.

Many professional sports players and athletes know exactly what their weight should be. Many professionals, such as players in the Premier League and tennis players (for example Rafael Nadal and Roger Federer) are likely to be heavier than other men of similar height as they are very well muscled.

Losing weight

Many people need to lose weight to reach their optimum weight. In some sports, such as boxing and horseracing, it is necessary to lose weight rapidly, as boxers and jockeys need to make the weight they are fighting or riding at.

People who want to lose weight usually do so by:

- decreasing calorie intake (dieting) or
- increasing calorie expenditure (exercise) or
- doing both (dieting plus exercise).

British boxer Frankie Gavin was sent home from the Beijing Olympics for being over the weight limit in his weight category.

21: Weight-related conditions

Objectives

At the end of this section you will be able to:

○ explain the terms anorexic, obese, overfat, overweight, underweight

○ explain how these conditions may affect physical activity.

A number of terms are used to describe medical conditions related to weight. The list includes:

◉ anorexic

◉ obese

◉ overfat

◉ overweight

◉ underweight.

Several of these conditions can result from a lack of physical activity.

Anorexic

Anorexia means 'without appetite' and is expressed as a desire not to become overfat or obese or a desire to become thin. Anorexia nervosa is a chronic illness which can be very dangerous. The loss of appetite can lead to extreme weight loss and result in a serious lack of nutrition, as well as psychological problems related to obsessions with food and calories.

> **edexcel ::: key terms**
>
> **Anorexic:** pertaining to anorexia – a prolonged eating disorder due to the loss of appetite.

Obese

Research has shown that obesity in the United Kingdom is increasing. Obesity carries considerable risks such as cancer and coronary heart disease (CHD), which can bring about heart attacks and strokes, as well as high blood pressure and type 2 diabetes. Studies have also shown that the incidence of obesity in children is increasing. It is thought that this is just as likely to be due to lack of exercise as eating too much of the wrong foods.

Obese people are unlikely to achieve sustained physical activity without much motivation. Extra weight makes exercise difficult and uncomfortable. As a result, obese people are not very likely to take part in sustained physical activity. However, exercise is an essential part of tackling obesity.

> **edexcel ::: key terms**
>
> **Obese:** a term used to describe people who are very overfat.

Apply it!

Go to the website: www. ahealthyme.com/topic/ waisthip.Take your measurements and use them to complete the table.

Overfat

The term overfat describes a physique which has an excessive fat content. It is often used to clarify the body type of somebody who is classified as overweight. For example, a woman who is overweight and has a high fat content would be described as overfat. However, a female weightlifter, who will probably be classified as overweight according to the BMI index, will not have such a high fat content and will therefore not be overfat.

edexcel key terms
Overfat: having body fat in excess of normal.

Overweight

There may be medical reasons why a person is overweight; in such cases, medical help is needed. Overweight is frequently associated with over-eating and inactivity. If an individual is eating more calories than they are using, their calories in will not equal calories out, resulting in an increase in weight. However, overweight can also refer to somebody whose body weight is greater than normal as a result of greater than normal muscle mass or a large bone structure.

Being overweight can often be beneficial to sportspeople as it means they have more muscle, which probably equals more strength. This applies to athletes such as wrestlers, javelin throwers, and rugby players. If a person is overweight but not involved in an activity of this type, they are less likely to perform well.

edexcel key terms
Overweight: having weight in excess of normal (not harmful unless accompanied by overfatness).

Underweight

Being underweight can affect performance. In some sports participants must fit into weight categories or weight limits. Boxing has had problems caused by participants losing weight to come within a certain weight limit, and this has sometimes been blamed for the boxers putting in a poor performance, being literally badly beaten. Flat race jockeys are often deliberately underweight for their height so they can ride at a prescribed weight for the horse.

How weight is lost is important. Boxers and jockeys may lose weight quickly by exercising and wearing sweat suits and/or taking steam baths to lose fluid through sweating which is not then replenished. Weight may also be lost by taking diuretic drugs. These are used to treat fluid retention; they work by making the person taking them urinate more frequently, thus causing weight loss through loss of fluid. All these methods of losing weight can cause dehydration, which impairs performance.

Some individuals may not be heavy enough for their sports and have to go on a special diet to put weight on, often by eating food which is high in calories. There may be medical reasons why a person is underweight, and in such cases medical help is needed.

edexcel key terms
Underweight: weighing less than is normal, healthy or required.

22: Performance-enhancing and recreational drugs

Objectives

By the end of this section you will:

○ know about the different categories of drugs: performance-enhancing and recreational

○ be able to explain the impact of performance-enhancing drugs on wellbeing and performance and why some performers might risk using them to enhance performance

○ be able to explain the effects of smoking and alcohol on general health and physical activity.

What is a drug? One definition states that a drug is a substance that can be taken in a variety of ways to produce expected and welcome physical and/or psychological effects on the person taking it, but may also cause some effects that are both unpleasant and unwanted. These are known as side effects.

There are two main categories of drugs:

◉ performance-enhancing

◉ recreational.

Side effects

All drugs have side effects. A side effect of some drugs is that they are addictive; this is as true of nicotine (cigarettes) and alcohol as it is of heroin and cocaine. If a person becomes addicted to using drugs it is often very difficult to give up.

Most drugs have physical side effects, which can range from high blood pressure to insomnia.

Performance-enhancing drugs

Performance-enhancing drugs can enhance a person's performance in some way, either in physical activity and training, or in daily life. They include some drugs that are socially acceptable and many that are illegal.

Performance-enhancing drugs include:

◉ anabolic steroids

◉ beta blockers

◉ diuretics

◉ narcotic analgesics

◉ stimulants

◉ peptide hormones including erythropoietin/EPO.

Why do people take performance-enhancing drugs?

Some people take drugs to enhance or improve their performance, or are encouraged to do so by their coaches or fellow athletes. The temptation to do this is great as the rewards of success can be high; winning an Olympic gold medal in some sports is said to be worth a million dollars in endorsements.

Professionals who compete at the highest levels can make a lot of money. Some athletes might take drugs so they can compete at a higher level than they would otherwise have reached.

Another incentive is that the competitive life of a professional sportsperson is comparatively short, and so they must become well-known enough and earn enough money to be able to live comfortably after their competitive life has finished.

In recent years it has been proved or alleged that competitors in cycling (the Tour de France), swimming, association football, weightlifting, American football, basketball, skiing, and the World's Strongest Man competition, as well as other sports, have taken drugs.

Anabolic steroids

Anabolic steroids are reputed to be the drugs most commonly used to enhance performance in sport. They mimic the male hormone testosterone and have the effects of deepening the voice and causing the growth of facial hair – side effects that are, of course, most noticeable in women. Anabolic steroids increase muscle mass and develop bone growth, therefore increasing strength while at the same time allowing the athlete to train harder and recover quicker. The other attraction is that they produce results quickly. Some people believe that the same effects can be gained legally using good training methods and correct nutrition.

Dwain Chambers, a British 100m sprinter found guilty of taking steroids, certainly benefited from using them. When he returned to athletics after being banned for two years, many experts debated whether his performance was still being enhanced as a result of the steroids he had taken, giving him an unfair advantage. His example made it clear that for a non-drugged athlete to beat a drugged athlete, the latter would have to be having 'a real bad day'.

Steroids also increase aggression. Some sportspeople take it mainly for this reason, although the drug is normally used to prevent muscle wastage and as an aid to rehabilitation.

The side effects of anabolic steroids include:

- increased risk of heart attacks and strokes

- high blood pressure

- liver disease

- increased risk of muscle injury

- infertility in women

- the worst case scenario – death.

Apply it!

Think of three different sports in which the development of muscular strength is very important and could help the sportsperson to win a gold medal.

edexcel ⠿ key terms

Anabolic steroids: drugs that mimic the male sex hormone testosterone and promote bone and muscle growth.

Beta blockers

These drugs are commonly prescribed for people with heart problems as they maintain a low heart rate and lower blood pressure. As a result stress levels and anxiety are reduced.

Beta blockers can help in target sports where steadiness and precision are required, because they reduce the heart rate. They are banned in many sports where steadiness is essential, such as snooker, archery, shooting, and curling, as well as in sports such as gymnastics and ski jumping, and control sports such as motor cycling. Beta blockers can reduce a fit person's heart rate to a dangerous level.

edexcel ⠿ key terms

Beta blockers: drugs that are used to control the heart rate and have a calming and relaxing effect.

The side effects of beta blockers include:

- nausea and diarrhoea
- tiredness
- depression
- insomnia and nightmares.

> **edexcel key terms**
> **Diuretics:** drugs that elevate the rate of urine production.

Diuretics

Diuretics are used to increase the amount of urine produced and to increase kidney function, so speeding up the elimination of fluid from the body. This can help performers who need to lose weight, e.g. boxers or jockeys. Diuretics may also be taken in an attempt to reduce the concentration of any other banned substance that may be present in the urine. The side effects of diuretics include:

- dehydration, which can cause dizziness, muscle cramps, headaches and nausea,
- and also long-term effects such as kidney problems.

Apply it!

Write down the names of three sports in which the performers may be tempted to use diuretics to lose weight quickly.

Narcotics/analgesics

Injuries can be a problem for many sportspeople. They want to compete, not sit and watch from the sidelines (and many of them make very poor spectators, especially in front of their own team mates). As a result, many are prepared to take drugs so they can return to competition as quickly as possible. Narcotics/analgesics help them do this. Drugs in this category include heroin, methadone, pethidine (for moderate pain), and the powerful painkiller, morphine.

These drugs act by depressing the central nervous system and give relief from painful injuries, but by allowing the injured player to take part, they can increase the risk of severe or long-lasting injury. This is one reason why they are banned; the other is that they can have dangerous side effects. Some are only available on prescription whereas some narcotics / analgesics are not legally available at all.

The side effects of narcotics/analgesics include:

- loss of concentration
- loss of balance
- loss of coordination
- emotional effects, including hallucinations (morphine).

> **edexcel key terms**
> **Narcotics analgesics:** drugs that can be used to reduce pain.

Stimulants

Stimulants are the second most commonly used drugs in sport. This group of drugs includes amphetamines, ephedrine, and cocaine (sometimes found in low doses in medicines for colds and pain relief), as well as nicotine and caffeine.

The latter two drugs are very common, and many people take them regularly. They increase alertness, enabling people to think more quickly by stimulating the central nervous system (CNS). Using these drugs helps to overcome tiredness. They are especially useful to offset the effects of lactic acid on muscles.

Cocaine is a recreational drug used by many professional sportspeople, including American footballers, baseball players, and boxers. Some professional footballers have also admitted using it.

> **edexcel key terms**
> **Stimulants:** drugs that have an effect on the central nervous system, such as increased mental and/or physical alertness.

The side effects of stimulants include:

- insomnia
- irritability
- irregular heart beat
- increased heart rate
- high blood pressure
- addiction – some stimulants, such as amphetamines, are highly addictive.

---

edexcel ⦂⦂⦂ key terms

Peptide hormones: drugs that cause other hormones to be produced.

Peptide hormones, including erythropoietin (EPO)

These drugs are often used to produce the same effects as anabolic steroids, namely, to increase muscle growth, and to assist in recovery from injury and heavy training sessions. The specific performance-enhancing quality of these drugs is that they increase the number of red blood cells, allowing the body to carry extra oxygen, and disperse waste products and lactic acid.

We all produce hormones naturally but they can also be produced synthetically by drugs. High doses are sometimes taken by athletes to increase muscle development. Human growth hormone (HGH) is now used by some athletes for this reason. Athletes are tested at regular intervals for the use of steroids, but HGH is a comparatively new drug that is being used to gain advantage. It is also thought to have fewer side effects than steroids. Although there is no urine test for HGH it can be detected through a blood test.

LINK IT UP!

To see how the cardiovascular system works go to CH 24.

Erythropoietin (EPO) is used to treat people with anaemia as it increases the production of red blood cells and therefore the amount of haemoglobin available to take up oxygen. This effect increases aerobic capacity, which is useful in, for example, longer distance events and cycle events.

One of the problems with EPO is that it thickens the blood, a condition which also occurs as a result of dehydration. This makes it much more difficult for blood to pass through the small capillaries and increases the risk of a heart attack or stroke. An accurate urine test has been in use since the 2004 Olympic Games in Athens to detect synthetic EPO.

Apply it!

Think of an example of an event where blood doping could be used to improve performance.

Drugs in sport

Taking illegal substances to improve performance goes back a long way. In 1952, it was reported that the USSR (the former Soviet Union) used androgenic anabolic steroids (testosterone) by injection to improve the performance of its weight lifters, and the USA followed suit.

It was not until the 1970s that the governing bodies began to make the use of drugs illegal and testing began. The International Olympic Commitee (IOC) first enforced a full scale testing programme for the 1972 Olympic Games in Munich, but anabolic steroids were not banned until 1975. In February 1999, at a conference in Lausanne, the IOC wanted agreement on two points:

1. a single international doping agency

2. a blanket two-year ban for competitors found guilty of drug taking.

The governing bodies of cycling, tennis, and football would not agree to the two-year ban but insisted on the inclusion of the words 'specific, exceptional circumstances'.

In some countries the testing procedures are not as strict as in others, and some countries do not take drug testing as seriously. For instance, although the British Olympic Association banned the 100m sprinter Dwain Chambers from taking part in the Olympics for life, many other countries would have allowed him to compete as he had already served a two-year ban.

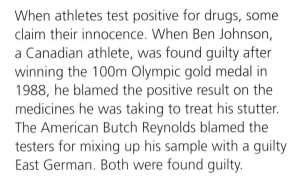

When athletes test positive for drugs, some claim their innocence. When Ben Johnson, a Canadian athlete, was found guilty after winning the 100m Olympic gold medal in 1988, he blamed the positive result on the medicines he was taking to treat his stutter. The American Butch Reynolds blamed the testers for mixing up his sample with a guilty East German. Both were found guilty.

The International Olympic Committee (IOC) which runs the Olympic Games has very strict rules on prohibited (banned) substances and methods. During the 2008 Beijing Olympics, Michael Phelps, an American swimmer who won eight gold medals, and Asafa Powell, a Jamaican 100m sprinter, both spoke about the high number of times they were tested before and during the games. In fact, Don Anderson, a member of Jamaica's Olympic association ascribed Powell's failure to win a medal – when he was expected to challenge Usain Bolt, a fellow Jamaican for gold – to the mental effect of so many tests.

Recreational drugs

Most people use recreational drugs on a regular basis. The obvious ones are caffeine, which can be found in tea, coffee, and some fizzy drinks; nicotine from smoking; and ethanol, more commonly known as alcohol.

Smoking and nicotine

Smoking has been banned in public places since 2007 and the legal age for buying tobacco products is now 18. Coronary heart disease (CHD), not cancer, is the commonest cause of death related to smoking. Smoking damages the cardiovascular system, in particular the heart, the oxygen-carrying capacity of the blood, and the blood vessels. It also causes high blood pressure. This has a negative effect on fitness, especially aerobic fitness, and often results in poorer performance.

Smoking just one cigarette can raise the heart rate. Medical operations carry a higher risk for smokers. Giving up smoking reduces these risks.

Nicotine, the drug contained in cigarettes, is a stimulant which raises alertness. As nicotine is an addictive drug, the more people smoke, the harder they find it to stop.

Alcohol

Alcohol is banned in some sports, such as shooting or archery, where it may be used as a sedative (have a calming effect). It is also banned in sports where it is considered a safety risk, such as motor sports, because it slows down reaction times and impairs judgment.

Alcohol can cause extra urine to be produced – as can caffeine – and this has to be disposed of, which increases the risk of dehydration. The long-term effects of alcohol include a form of liver damage known as cirrhosis.

Socially acceptable and unacceptable

Socially acceptable drugs are those that may be prescribed by a doctor or which can be bought over the counter, such as paracetamol and aspirin, to treat medical conditions.

Socially unacceptable drugs are illegal and unacceptable to most people. They include heroin, cocaine, LSD, amphetamines, barbiturates, cannabis and ecstasy. All of these have negative effects and can be dangerous, in some cases leading to death.

23: Risk assessment and preventing injuries

Objectives

By the end of this section you will be able to identify the risks associated with participation in physical activities and explain how to reduce these risks with special consideration to:

- warming up / cooling down
- checking equipment and facilities
- correct clothing
- balanced competition
- playing within the rules of competition

understand the need for a physical activity readiness questionnaire (PAR-Q) to reduce risk when participating in physical activity.

Most physical activities and sports have some element of risk attached to them, although this will be higher in some cases than others, both in terms of an accident happening and the severity of the possible injury. However, much can be done to minimise risk.

Warming up / cooling down

One of the main reasons for warming up is that warming the muscles gradually helps to prevent injury. Remember that cooling down serves not to prevent injury but to disperse lactic acid. preventing soreness and aches.

Checking equipment and facilities

Organisers and officials, as well as participants, need to check for safety before an activity or competition. Organisers should check that the facilities are safe and secure, and that any equipment is in good condition. The specific checks needed will of course vary considerably according to the activity. Before a football match, for example, officials must check that the pitch is suitable to play on and that the markings are clearly visible.

Protective equipment and clothing

Many activities call for protective equipment and clothing and some, such as football, hockey, sailing, and riding, have the need for such equipment built into the rules. The clothing may also vary according to the position you play. Hockey goalkeepers wear more protective clothing than the rest of the team, and the same is true of a batsman in cricket. It is quite easy to explain why these players need extra protection, as they play in positions where they are vulnerable to being hit by a very hard ball which is travelling at speed.

It is also important not to wear clothing that might injure an opponent (or team mate).

Jewellery should preferably be removed or taped over if it cannot be removed.

edexcel ⋮⋮⋮ examiner tip

In the exam you should choose the most obvious answer to questions about the avoidance of injury in specific sports.

Apply it!

With a partner or in your group produce a list of four sports together with their appropriate clothing and equipment. Pick sports from different categories e.g. team contact sport, individual contact sport, racket sport, and individual non-contact sport. Set your answer out as a table.

Footwear

One of most important items of equipment is footwear; most sports require specialist shoes or boots. Apart from helping performance, it is always safer to wear the correct footwear. In contact invasion games it is easy to see why this is so: football boots have studs to give grip. Sprinters need sprinting spikes for better grip to help them run faster and so perform better, but they can also injure other athletes if they tread on their feet. Jumpers, especially triple jumpers, need extra protection in their shoes for when they land, particularly in the hop phase. Footwear which is worn for safety reasons must not be damaged. Before a Premier League football player is allowed on to the pitch their football boots must be checked for damage to the studs.

Road runners need special footwear as pounding the roads takes its toll on the feet, ankles, knees, and hip joints, as well as the leg muscles, especially the gastrocnemius. Shoes are the most important part of a runner's equipment, and must be chosen carefully as each foot lands about 800 times in every mile. Running shoes can be very expensive as a lot of research goes into producing them; choosing the right ones is very important for comfort and support.

Apply it!

Name an activity of your choice and list the equipment you would need for a typical training session. Choose an obvious activity that you find easy to write about.

110

Balanced competition

When creating a balanced and fair competition, numerous factors need to be considered.

Weight categories

In sports such as boxing, the competitors are matched according to their weight as well as ability. This is necessary to protect participants' safety: a 7ft, 20 stone professional boxer obviously cannot safely take on another boxer who is 5ft tall and weighs 8 stone. Weight lifting is divided into weight divisions in order to equalise competition, but not for safety purposes. Karate and judo, on the other hand, are examples of activities that have clearly defined skill levels and where players take part according to their ability.

Mixed or single sex

In most sports, men play against men and women against women. This is for reasons of safety especially in contact sports. Netball, hockey, football, cricket, and rugby are examples. Athletics and swimming are also divided by sex on grounds of fair competition, although not necessarily on grounds of safety. Some invasion games, such as hockey, can be played as mixed sex. Racket games such as tennis, badminton and table tennis can be played as mixed doubles and give a clear opportunity for men and women to compete fairly in open competition.

Age

Competitive sport for very young children has been a controversial issue for some time and some people think that too much competition at an early age is bad for children. Children's competitions are normally in age groups but talented performers do sometimes play out of their age group. In terms of safety, overuse injuries are frequent among young athletes. Although, being grouped by age does not guarantee that the players will be of equal height and weight and that 'little ones' do not play against 'big ones' in the same age group.

At the other end of the scale, some sports can be played in veteran or senior categories, quite often for safety reasons. Veterans compete in team games such as football, netball, tennis, badminton, table tennis, and rugby, and also in individual sports such as golf. Many veterans take part in the London Marathon; some of them even into their 90s.

Handicap system

Another way to balance competition is to use a handicap system. This is used in golf; it is a way of ensuring that players of unequal ability can play in direct competition with each other.

Playing to the rules of competition

All games and sports have rules so that there can be fair competition. Rules help to ensure safety and help games to flow. If rules are broken participants are punished, which may rarely mean a lifetime ban.

Occasionally in sport 'professional fouls' – where players deliberately act to stop or affect play – are used, particularly in team games. Behaviour like this goes against the spirit of 'fair play'. Over-aggression or professional fouls can cause serious injuries which could threaten a player's career. Players can be heavily fined and/or banned for over-aggressive play outside the rules and 'spirit of the game'.

LINK IT UP!

See CH 10 for more information on the PAR-Q.

Physical readiness

Anyone who is going to start a personal exercise programme or take part in physical activity must first make sure they are ready to do so. The physical activity readiness questionnaire (PAR-Q) needs to be answered, and a medical examination is also advisable. This preparation should highlight any potential problems that could determine which activity to choose and how often to take part.

edexcel ⠿ key terms

PAR-Q: physical activity readiness questionnaire.

ResultsPlus
Build Better Answers

All sporting activities have clearly stated rules. State three reasons why we have rules in sport. (June 2008, 3 marks)

Answer

1. protect players from injury/increase safety/equivalent

2. increase the enjoyment/fun of the activity (players/ spectators)/encourage good sporting behaviour/ maintain control/prevent arguments/equivalent

3. so the game is fair/so there is no cheating/equivalent

4. give the game structure/identify winners/better competition/equivalent.

Any order was acceptable. Although only 1 point per category of answer was credited. Reference to balanced competition/ technique/to discipline players was not accepted.

Examiner's comment

This question was well answered in 2008. The main three different responses related to: fun, fairness and safety. Candidates need to able to give a range of responses to gain maximum marks for this question.

examzone

Know Zone
Topic 1.2.1: Physical activity and your healthy mind and body

In this topic you will learn about a variety of things that are concerned with the body and its structure, and body composition. Body composition is about the percentage of body weight that is fat, muscle and bone. It varies from person to person and is affected by gender, height, bone size and muscle girth. This influences somatotype, which in turn influences the sports – or even specific positions – we are most likely to be good at.

Other terms are also covered that affect some people's lifestyle today, from anorexia to obesity and how optimum weight may vary and be influenced by a variety of things. Performance-enhancing and recreational drugs are also covered.

You should know...

- [ ] The different body types (somatotypes): endomorph, mesomorph, ectomorph.
- [ ] The effect each can have on participation and performance
- [ ] Be able to identify activities where different body types are an advantage.
- [ ] Understand optimum weight, why it varies according to height, gender, bone structure and muscle girth, and how it can affect performance and participation in physical activity.

You should also be able to explain:

- [ ] the terms anorexic, obese, overfat, overweight, underweight
- [ ] how these conditions may affect physical activity
- [ ] risk assessment, kit, equipment, readiness, rules, clothing and balanced competition

Examiner's tip

You need to know the names of the somatotypes, the body build/shape of each, and the type of sporting activities with which they are predominantly associated. You also need to understand the terms overweight, overfat and obese. You should be able to explain that in some sports performers may be overweight because they are heavily muscled and that this is not a problem, although overfat, where too much of the person's body composition is fat, can be.

Key terms

Somatotype

Mesomorph

Anorexic

Overfat

Underweight

Balanced competition

Endomorph

Ectomorph

Obese

Overweight

Performance-enhancing drugs

Stretch activity

Measure your somatotype and plot it on a somato chart. Discuss the implications of body type on your main sport, or the position you play in that sport. Think why men and women should have separate charts. Discuss how the terms anorexia, overweight, underweight and obesity fit with body types and how drugs can influence body type and shape.

Support activity

Compare the rules and equipment and safety requirements in different sports, e.g. age groups, weight of throwing equipment in athletics. Compare the performance-enhancing drugs different sportspeople might take. What would they hope to achieve and how might they be punished if caught?

Question:
Complete the table.

(i) Name the body type of each performer.
(ii) State one reason why this body type is an advantage to the performer in his/her sport. (Total 6 marks)

PERFORMER	(i) BODY TYPE	(ii) REASON FOR ADVANTAGE
SPRINTER		
TENNIS PLAYER		
HIGH JUMPER		

Students' answer	Examiners' comments	Build Better Answers
(i) Sprinter = endomorph Tennis player = endomorph High jumper = endomorph	⚠ This is wrong. Some students, like this one, mixed up the somatotypes and this means they will lose at least two marks. In these questions students either know the answer or not; there is no room for anything other than the correct term.	Sprinter = mesomorph Tennis player = mesomorph High jumper = ectomorph
(ii) Sprinter = endomorph – can run faster Tennis player = endomorph – can run faster High jumper = endomorph – can jump higher	◼ Some students identified the wrong somatotype and some did not give a reason that was valid e.g. high jump: ectomorph: is lighter but did not explain how this was an advantage. A better answer would have been that ectomorphs have less weight to get over the bar-taller so higher centre of gravity. Students who identified the somatotype incorrectly could not give a valid reason; e.g. if they said endomorph the reason 'they run faster' cannot be valid as it is not true of that body type.	Sprinter = mesomorph – strong and powerful which helps to get a good start driving out of the starting blocks and run faster. Tennis player = mesomorph – strong and powerful so they can hit the ball harder. High jumper = ectomorph – usually tall and lighter with a higher centre of gravity, lighter in weight to get up and over the bar.

Examiner's comment
In these questions students must make sure that they give a reason, not just say the mesomorph is stronger or the ectomorph is taller – how does this help? This was a disappointing question in terms of how well the students performed with fewer than 20% gaining 3 marks for the explain part and only 46% for identifying the somatotypes.

Practice Exam Questions

(i) Which of the following three body conditions is considered to be the most dangerous to our health? (1)

A Obese   B Overfat   C Overweight

(ii) Why is it **unlikely** that an elite performer will have this condition? (1)

(iii) Some elite performers, for example rugby players, will weigh more than their 'expected' weight, but still be the appropriate weight for their sport. Why will these performers weigh more than expected? (1)

Competitions are often balanced.
 (i) Explain the term balanced competition. (1)   (ii) State three ways that competition can be balanced. (3)

Topic 1.2.2: A healthy, active lifestyle and your cardiovascular system

Sport in Context

Jogging raises the heart rate and makes the heart beat harder. This change during exercise is all part of the cardiovascular system's job, helping the body to cope with the demands of physical activities. Professional athletes like Rebecca Adlington, the Olympic swimmer, have very fit hearts which pump more blood through the body, more quickly and more efficiently.

The cardiovascular system consists of the heart, the blood and the blood vessels. Exercising affects all these parts, not just the heart, and in this topic you will learn how the cardiovascular system works and how it is affected by training. You will learn how to take your heart rate to monitor your cardiovascular fitness. Finally, you will see how the cardiovascular system can be affected by drugs.

PE and me

1. Can you name some exercises which make your heart beat faster?

2. Why do you think the heart needs to beat faster during exercise?

3. Can you think of different, non-sporting moments, when your heart beats faster than normal?

4. Do you know what the average person's resting heart rate is? Why will a professional athlete's be lower than this?

Topic Overview

By the end of this topic you will be able to:

- describe the cardiovascular system

- explain the immediate effects of exercise, and the long-term benefits of regular exercise, on the cardiovascular system

- explain how rest, diet, and drugs affect the cardiovascular system.

24: The cardiovascular system during exercise

Objectives

After this chapter you should understand:

- the immediate and short-term effects of participation in exercise and physical activity including:
  - increased heart rate
  - systolic/diastolic blood pressure
  - increased blood pressure

What is the cardiovascular system?

The cardiovascular system consists of the heart, blood and the blood vessels.

- The heart is a muscular pump, which pushes blood throughout the many blood vessels in the body.

- Blood being pushed around the body by the heart has two main functions:

  1. to supply the body with oxygen and nutrients

  2. to remove waste products such as carbon dioxide.

- The blood vessels that run throughout the body allow the blood to travel everywhere.

A strong cardiovascular system often means good cardiovascular fitness. This is the ability to exercise the entire body for long periods of time. To do this you need a **strong heart**, and **clear blood vessels** (arteries and veins) to supply the muscles with plenty of oxygen via the **blood**. Cardiovascular fitness is not just important to all sports people, but to everyone, because it needs the fitness of the most important **muscle** in the body - the heart!

116

What happens to the cardiovascular system during exercise?

Exercise has a number of immediate effects upon the cardiovascular system.

Increased heart rate

Heart rate is the number of times the heart beats per minute. Heart rate can vary considerably from person to person. Therefore it is difficult to say what a normal heart rate is. However, normal resting heart rate is accepted to be between 60–80 beats per minute (bpm); 72bpm is often regarded as average.

Exercise makes the body work harder. As a result, the muscles require more oxygen, which means the body needs more oxygen and more nutrients, such as glycogen, to function properly. Oxygen and nutrients are carried to the muscles by the blood. Therefore the heart has to work faster to pump blood around the body. This means that the heart rate (beats per minute) increases.

To bring about a change in heart rate the body releases **adrenaline**, which is the main cause of changes in heart rate and blood pressure. Adrenaline is a hormone. It makes the heart beat faster and, among other things, causes glycogen to be released by the liver, and blood to be diverted away from the organs (liver, kidney, and brain) to the muscles, which need to work harder during exercise.

After eating, more blood is sent to the digestive organs to carry nutrients to the muscles. Adrenaline diverts blood away from the digestive organs and this is one reason why it is not a good idea to exercise after eating a large meal.

Stressful situations, such as an important competition, can also cause adrenaline to be released.

There will be no questions in the exam on adrenaline but knowing about it will help you understand what brings about the increase in heart rate during exercise.

edexcel ::: key terms

Heart rate (pulse rate): the number of times the heart beats per minute

Blood pressure: the force exerted by circulating blood on the walls of the blood vessels

LINK IT UP!

A reason for taking part in physical activity is to relieve stress, see CH 2.

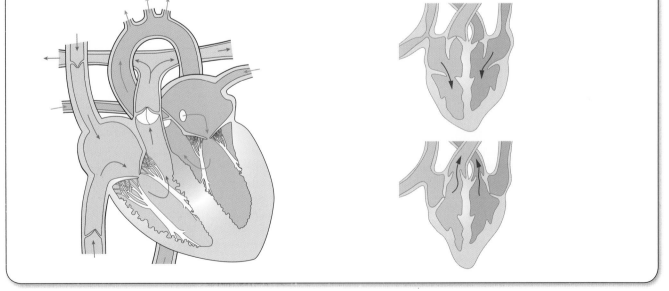

Cross-section of heart and illustration showing the contractions that take place to push blood in, then out of the heart through the blood vessels.

Blood pressure

The heart makes two beating sounds. The first is called systole, and is made by the lower chambers contracting and pushing blood at high pressure into the arteries. The actual sound is caused by the heart valves closing. The second sound is called diastole and is made by the upper chambers contracting, pushing blood down into the lower chambers. During exercise these sounds get louder, mainly as a result of an increase in blood pressure.

Increased blood pressure

Blood pressure is the force exerted by blood on the walls of the arteries. It increases during exercise because more blood is pumped around the body, increasing pressure on the blood vessels.

A blood pressure meter is used to measure systolic and diastolic blood pressure.

Systolic/diastolic pressure

● Systolic blood pressure is the maximum pressure in the arteries when the heart contracts (beats) and pushes blood out through the aorta into the body. It rises during activity or excitement as more blood is required by the body. It falls during sleep when the body is at rest.

● Diastolic blood pressure is the pressure of the blood during the relaxation phase between heart beats (when the heart is at rest). It depends mainly on the elasticity of the arteries and quality of the vessels.

● Pulse pressure is the difference between systolic and diastolic blood pressures.

Abnormal blood pressure

Systolic	persistently above 140mmHg
Diastolic	persistently above 85 mmHg
Pulse pressure	constantly above 50 or below 30

What can I do to reduce the risk of high blood pressure?

There is a lot that can be done to help to keep blood pressure at a normal level.

1. Check your weight.
2. Limit your alcohol consumption.
3. Don't smoke! Smoking damages the heart and blood vessels and raises blood pressure.
4. Eating too much salt may unbalance body chemistry and affect blood pressure.
5. Try to avoid situations which cause stress, anxiety or worry.
6. Regular exercise helps to control stress, keep blood pressure normal, and keep the whole system in good shape.

Immediate physiological effects of exercise on the body

1. Breathing becomes faster and deeper

Breathing gets faster and deeper so more oxygen can be supplied to the lungs. However fast the heart beats, it cannot carry enough oxygen if the lungs are not being supplied with enough through efficient breathing. Breathing efficiently means removing enough oxygen from the air.

LINK IT UP!

The most important structures in oxygen uptake are the alveoli. Topic 1.2.3 contains more information about these and about how their function can be impaired.

Apply it!

List three activities or times during an activity when you may become breathless.

2. Body temperature increases

During exercise the muscles work and generate heat, which causes body temperature to rise. The average temperature in humans is 37°C (98.6°F); between 36.4 and 37.2 are accepted as normal limits. Body temperature is regulated by heat radiating from the skin and water evaporating through sweating. Shivering means the muscles are working to produce heat in order to raise body temperature.

3. Sweating starts and body requires fluids

As the body temperature rises during exercise, sweating begins. The body tolerates a small rise in temperature, but at a certain point it will try to cool down and begin to sweat. Sweat comes out of the pores of the skin, and evaporates when it reaches the surface.

Apply it!

List three sports in which drinks are taken at regular intervals.

Energy, in the form of heat, is needed for it to evaporate, and this comes from the body. As heat is lost, body temperature falls. Salt as well as water is lost through sweating, and this can cause problems.

Under normal conditions, water content is controlled.

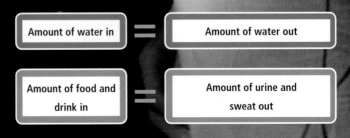

Amount of water in	=	Amount of water out
Amount of food and drink in	=	Amount of urine and sweat out

If the conditions are hot, sweating increases, and less urine is produced. Salt lost through sweating must be replaced so that the balance of salt in the body stays the same, otherwise cramp may occur.

Lack of water and salt can result in fainting or collapsing, which in certain sports are not uncommon; for example, long boxing matches in high temperatures. Football, tennis, and cycling are examples of activities where participants need to drink regularly.

At marathons, regular feeding stations provide the runners with energy drinks or plain water to prevent dehydration (drying out) and cramp. This is why refreshments must be taken both before and during the early stages of the race.

4. Muscles begin to ache

In order to work, muscles need energy and oxygen. Energy comes from food which is mainly converted to glucose (sugar). Glucose and oxygen are carried to the muscles by the blood. Wastes such as carbon dioxide are carried away by the blood. This process of getting energy is called respiration.

When muscles do extra work more glucose and oxygen are needed, so more blood must flow to the muscles and the heart must beat faster. The blood vessels narrow to raise the pressure, so extra blood can be sent to the muscles instead of to the organs of the body. Eventually it becomes impossible to get enough oxygen to the muscles, so they use a different method of getting energy. This is called anaerobic respiration. Glucose is still used, but a waste product called lactic acid is also produced.

Apply it!

Which two fuels are required to give energy to muscles?

119

Lactic acid

Lactic acid is a poison. It builds up slowly during exercise up to 75 per cent of maximum work rate, but, during higher intensity work, it builds up in the muscles much more quickly. The reason for this is usually poor training. It can also be a result of the depletion of glycogen stores in the muscles as a result of massive muscular effort, such as might occur in extra time of a hard football match played in muddy conditions, or in a marathon. After a while lactic acid will make the muscles ache. It will eventually cause cramp, and the muscles will stop working. The athlete has to rest while the blood brings fresh supplies of oxygen.

Producing energy with oxygen is called **aerobic respiration**.

Producing energy without oxygen is called **anaerobic respiration**.

LINK IT UP!

Explanations of aerobic and anaerobic are in CH 15.

25: Regular exercise and the cardiovascular system

Objectives

○ By the end of this chapter you should be able to explain the effects of regular and long-term participation in exercise and physical activity.

edexcel ⊞ key terms

Cardiac output: the amount of blood ejected from the heart in one minute

Stroke volume: the volume of blood pumped out of the heart by each ventricle during one contraction

Regular or long-term participation in physical activity has many benefits, the most important of which is that the heart becomes more efficient.

The effect of regular exercise on the cardiovascular system

Decreased resting heart rate
The resting heart rate gives an indication of fitness. This is because the heart gets bigger and stronger with training, so it can supply the same amount of blood with fewer beats. Therefore the heart of a fit persons beats fewer times, which is more efficient and results in less stress on the heart.

Heart recovery rate
Heart recovery rate is the speed at which the heart returns to normal after exercise. The faster the recovery rate, the fitter the person. A fast heart recovery rate is another long-term benefit of exercise.

Increased stroke volume
Stroke volume is the amount of blood pumped by the heart per beat. When a person exercises regularly, stroke volume increases, both at rest and at work. This is because the heart becomes more efficient and stronger as a result of regular training. At rest, stroke volume may be 85ml but when exercising it could be up to 130ml.

Cardiac output
Cardiac output is the amount of blood ejected from the heart in one minute. It is governed by the heart rate (pulse) and the stroke volume, which both change when a person participates in exercise over a long time. The equation to calculate cardiac output is:

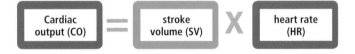

Cardiac output (CO) = stroke volume (SV) X heart rate (HR)

A trained athlete, such as Olympic 400 metres champion Christine Ohuruogu, could have a resting pulse rate as low as 40 BPM, while an average person might have a resting pulse rate of 72 BPM. The resting pulse rate can also be affected by age, sex, size, posture, eating, emotion, body temperature, environmental factors and smoking.

Blood pressure

Regular exercise reduces blood pressure. Exercise can help with weight loss, which can reduce blood pressure: being overweight can cause/add to the risk of having high blood pressure. Although it is possible to have high blood pressure without knowing, it can lead to a stroke or heart attack.

Factors which can affect blood pressure in individuals include age, sex, muscular development, stress, and tiredness. Altitude can also affect blood pressure, as the body reacts to the low oxygen pressure which can occur at high altitudes.

Healthy veins and arteries

Fitness increases the number of capillaries within the heart muscle. It also helps to make blood vessels more flexible and efficient, and so to stay clear.

Regular exercise can help weight loss and reduce blood pressure.

If a heart attack occurs, the area of damage is critical. A blockage in a fit person's blood vessel is likely to result in less damage than it might in an unfit person. This is another long-term benefit of exercise.

Causes of coronary heart disease (CHD)

Heart disease causes more deaths in the developed world than any other disease.

The causes of heart disease include hereditary conditions, infections, narrowing of the coronary arteries, high blood pressure, and of course smoking. The most common form of heart disease in the UK is atherosclerosis, which is caused by deposits of fat and cholesterol on the inside walls of the arteries. People who suffer from this condition are often short of breath, especially after exercise, and may suffer from chest pains, which are called angina. The condition causes an increase in blood pressure (which is a good reason for checking blood pressure regularly), resulting from narrowing of the arteries which impedes the flow of blood. (Imagine pinching the end of a garden hose pipe when the water is pumping through it.) This can lead to a heart attack.

To recap, the benefits of regular exercise include:

1. heart pumps more blood per beat (increased stroke volume) and becomes more efficient

2. lower resting pulse

3. return to resting pulse rate quicker (recovery rate)

4. lower blood pressure

5. veins and arteries become healthier reducing the risk of coronary heart disease

6. size and volume of heart increases

7. resting heart rate is reduced, lowering work load on the heart

26: The effect of lifestyle on the cardiovascular system

Objectives

By the end of this chapter you should understand and be able to explain:

- the need for rest and recovery time
- the impact of diet on the cardiovascular system, in particular how it can effect blood pressure and cholesterol (HDL and LDL)
- the effects of recreational drugs.

edexcel ⠿ key terms

Rest: The period of time allotted to recovery

Rest

Rest is essential to recovery and to allow the body to adapt. Specifically, rest allows the heart to grow in size and thickness and the number of capillaries to increase. An example of a good training programme with rest would be two days training, followed by a rest day, then three days training, followed by another rest day. In total this is five exercise sessions of 30 minutes and two days rest a week.

LINK IT UP!

The principle of rest is also covered in the principles of training CH 11.

Factors that may have a negative effect on the cardiovascular system and increase the risk of coronary heart disease

1. High cholesterol, perhaps due to a diet high in animal fats

2. Recreational drugs

3. Sedentary lifestyle and lack of exercise (hypokinetic disease)

4. Stress.

1. High cholesterol

Cholesterol is a fatty substance carried in the blood by lipoproteins. Lipoproteins come in two forms:

- High density lipoprotein (HDL) contains more protein than fat and is referred to as 'good cholesterol' because it carries cholesterol away from the arteries to the liver, which removes it from the body. Foods rich in HDL include fruit, vegetables, whole grains, and legumes (e.g. peas and beans). This is one reason to include five portions of fruit and vegetables in the daily diet.

- Low density lipoprotein (LDL) consists mainly of fat and is known as ' bad cholesterol'. It is the major cause of cholesterol in the blood, and can lead to a build-up of plaque which can restrict blood flow in the arteries. Blockages in the blood vessels mean that the heart has to work harder to pump blood around the body, resulting in an increase in blood pressure.

A clear artery

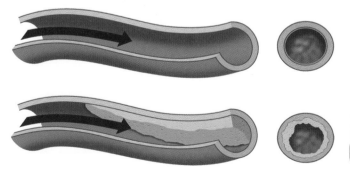

Plaque build up in an artery

High cholesterol can be caused by a diet high in LDL, such as saturated fat (bad fat). Cholesterol only becomes a problem when the level in the blood is too high. More cholesterol than the body needs can cause a build up of fatty deposits (plaque) in the arteries and lead to heart problems. This can increase the risk of coronary heart disease as well as narrowing of the arteries and consequently heart attacks.

ResultsPlus
Build Better Answers

These questions relate to the effects of exercise on the cardiovascular system. For each question decide whether A, B, C or D is correct. (Total 3 marks)

A   statement true, example true

B   statement true, example false

C   statement false and example true

D   statement false and example false

	Statement	Example
(a)	Regular training has an effect on the circulatory system.	An increase in heart rate
(b)	An immediate effect of exercise is an increase in heart rate	Heart rate increases from 65 bpm to 75 bpm
(c)	Regular exercise has no long-term benefit on the cardiovascular system	Lower resting heart rate

Examiner's comment: Firstly you should read the information in the table. So, start by reading the statements, if you think they are true put a tick in the box, or if you think they are wrong put a cross. Then do the same for the examples. Then look at the statements and the example and see which potential answer A, B, C or D is matched.

124

edexcel ::: examiner tip
Remember that nicotine is a drug, not cigarettes.

2. Recreational drugs

These include cigarettes (nicotine), which raise blood pressure because they release adrenaline. Adrenaline constricts the arteries and causes the heart to beat faster.

Tobacco smoke is a major risk factor of heart disease. Smoking lowers HDL cholesterol ('good' cholesterol) levels and increases the tendency for blood to clot, which can lead to serious problems such as heart attacks or strokes.

Alcohol in moderation is thought to increase HDL and so in the long term can help to lower blood pressure. However, too much alcohol and binge drinking can have serious adverse affects.

Some people have to take prescription drugs to control their blood pressure. Others may be prescribed drugs which actually cause high blood pressure for other medical conditions; these people may be prescribed additional drugs to control their blood pressure.

3. Sedentary lifestyle and lack of exercise

Inactivity means that the cardiovascular system does not receive the benefits of exercise. Sedentary living is also believed to be one of the main reasons for increasing rates of obesity.

4. Stress

The stress that may increase the risk of cardiovascular disease is different to the stress felt before a competition or while taking an exam. Negative stress builds up over time and can affect the cardiovascular system by leading to an increase in blood pressure and elevated heart rate. It may also lead to depression and mood swings.

Summary

Cardiovascular exercise and improvements in cardiovascular fitness can reduce the risk of these factors because they reduce the risk of coronary heart disease. Exercise improves the cardiovascular system, and helps to reduce blood pressure. The earlier topics showed how it helps to reduce stress and burn off excess calories. People who are keen to get fit will probably be motivated not to smoke, this is a long-term effect of exercise. Over a period of time, the heart of a fit person will beat far fewer times. This makes it much more efficient and causes less stress to be put on the heart, another long-term benefit of exercise.

With training, the heart muscle increases in size, thickness and strength, the chambers increase in volume, and the whole heart gets bigger, allowing it to work harder for longer; another long-term benefit of exercise.

Apply it!

1. Write out in your own words what is meant by cardiovascular fitness.

2. Suggest three ways in which you can improve cardiovascular fitness.

3. Name three activities where high levels of cardiovascular fitness would be crucial to performance.

ResultsPlus
Build Better Answers

Ali plays badminton for the school team but is frightened of losing his place due to his lack of fitness. He has decided to plan a Personal Exercise Programme (PEP) to help him improve his fitness for badminton. (June 2005, 2 marks)

State TWO long-term benefits you would expect Ali's training to have on his cardiovascular system. (2)

Answer:

Lower blood pressure/increase stroke volume/max cardiac output/drop in resting heart rate/ heart gets stronger
'Heart gets bigger' would be incorrect

Examiner's Comment:

Candidates identified that stroke volume increases, or that the heart gets stronger, but there appeared to be little reference to any of the other training effects. You should make sure you understand the effects of exercise on blood pressure: an acceptable answer relating to this would be 'lower blood pressure'.

examzone

Know Zone

Topic 1.2.2: A healthy, active lifestyle and your cardiovascular system

In this topic you will learn how your lifestyle affects your cardiovascular system, what happens when you are exercising, and the effects of exercising over a short period of time, for example when performing your 6-week PEP, and on a regular basis over a long period of time.

You should know...

- ☐ The impact of a healthy active lifestyle on your cardiovascular system.
- ☐ The immediate and short-term effects of participation in exercise and physical activity.
- ☐ The effects of regular and long-term participation in exercise and physical activity.
- ☐ The need for rest and recovery time.
- ☐ About diet and the cardiovascular system, HDL and LDL.
- ☐ The effects of recreational drugs.

Examiner's tip

Keep any graphical analysis of your exercise sessions during your PEP and the tests you performed in respect of your cardiovascular system at the start and at the end. Analysing these when you have completed your PEP will help you to evaluate how your training went. Apply your knowledge of how your PEP affected your cardiovascular system.

Key terms

Heart rate
Resting heart rate
Working heart rate
Recovery rate
Blood pressure
HDL and LDL
Cardiac output
Stroke volume
Rest

Stretch activity

Keep the graphs of any exercise sessions you may have recorded for your PEP. These should show your resting, working and recovery heart rates. Compare them; has your resting heart rate fallen over a period of time? Record your resting heart regularly, for example first thing on each Sunday morning during your 6-week PEP. Compare the results over the 6-week period.

Support activity

You could take photographs while you are exercising and put them into your PEP. An example might be a photograph of you looking at your heart rate monitor after completing a Cooper's 12 minute run test. You will have a record of your heart rate and the photograph; this will indicate an immediate effect of exercise and you should be able to explain it.

Question: (i) Which of the following best describes cardiac output? (1)
The amount of times your heart beats per minute.
The amount of blood leaving the heart per minute.
The amount of blood leaving the heart per beat.
The amount of blood leaving the heart per breath.

(ii) What effects will long term training have on the heart muscle and the chambers of the heart? (1)

(iii) What effect will long term training have on your resting heart rate and stroke volume? (2)
(Heart rate (1) Stroke volume (1))

Students' answer	Examiners' comments	Build Better Answers
(i) Student A: The amount of times the heart beats per minute. Student B: The amount of blood leaving the heart per beat.	Student A got the wrong answer and confused heart rate and cardiac output. Student B answered incorrectly as well. Most candidates got this question wrong. These are the questions that you must get right if you are to get an A*–C.	The answer was: the amount of blood leaving the heart per minute.
(ii) Student A: It will pump more blood around per beat. Student B: It will improve his cardiovascular system.	Student A is correct. Student B is incorrect. The question was specific to the part of the heart and increasing or pumping more blood.	Alternative correct answers would be: increased strength/size/stronger. Increase strength of contraction/ pump more blood/increase stroke volume.
(iii) Student A: Heart rate – Lowers. Stroke volume – higher. Student B: Resting heart rate increases. Stroke volume – more blood could be produced.	Student A is correct. Student B got both wrong. The resting heart rate decreases and more blood is not produced but more blood is pumped. 44% of students failed to get 2/2 for this question. These are questions you can learn and apply when you are creating your PEP.	Resting heart rate decreases and stroke volume increases.

It is essential to learn and understand the key terms on the cardiovascular system and their definitions.
It will help if you put them in practical context and evaluate results. You can do this in your PEP.

Practice Exam Questions

1 During a game, players will work at varying intensities. Sometimes they will be walking or jogging, at other times they will need to sprint.

(i) What happens to the players' heart rates as they change workload? (1)

(ii) This change in activity would have a similar effect on cardiac output. What is cardiac output? (1)

(iii) Why is it important to a performer that cardiac output changes when exercising at varying intensities? (1)

Topic 1.2.3: A healthy, active lifestyle and your respiratory system

Sport in Context

Christine Ohuruogu is leading in the 400 metres final at the Olympics Games. As the runners come down the home straight they are all gasping for breath. What is going on in their respiratory systems?

This topic describes what happens to the respiratory system during exercise and after exercise when you are left gasping for breath. You will learn about the immediate and short-term effects of exercise on your respiratory system, the need for extra oxygen during exercise, and the build up of oxygen debt. You will look at the effects of regular exercise and long-term participation in physical activity on the respiratory system, as well as the effects of rest and smoking.

PE and me

1. What do you know about the respiratory system and what it does?

2. Why do you think athletes in events such as the 400 metres are gasping for breath when they finish?

3. Do all athletes breathe as heavily after an event or training session?

4. Have you ever felt breathless after exercise? What were you doing?

Topic Overview

By the end of this topic you will be able to:

- describe the respiratory system and what happens to it during exercise

- explain the effects of regular exercise on the respiratory system

- understand how recreational drugs can affect the respiratory system.

27: The respiratory system

Objectives

When you have finished this chapter you will understand the main function of the respiratory system and respiration.

During exercise, the body needs to take in a sufficient supply of oxygen and eliminate the carbon dioxide produced by the muscles while they are working. Oxygen is breathed in and carbon dioxide breathed out in a process known as gaseous exchange. An efficient respiratory system allows more oxygen to reach the blood and consequently the muscles. This is important because the harder and longer (intensity and time) the physical activity, the more oxygen is needed to keep the muscles working and the more carbon dioxide produced.

Working very hard may result in the body needing more oxygen than it can get. This is known as **oxygen debt**. It could occur, for example, at the end of a 400 metres race or a hard sprint in a game situation.

After intense exercise athletes often gasp for air.

How the respiratory system works

When breathing in (inhaling), the intercostal muscles (the muscles between the ribs) contract and lift the chest upwards and outwards while the diaphragm (a sheet of muscle which separates the chest region from the rest of the body cavity) tightens and lowers. These actions open the lungs and create a vacuum inside so that air (with oxygen) can rush in through the nose and mouth, where it is warmed, moistened and filtered.

The air passes through the trachea (the tube that takes air into the chest) and one of the two bronchi into the left or the right lung. After passing through the many bronchioles (smaller tubes) it arrives into some of the millions of tiny sacs called alveoli which are surrounded by capillaries (very narrow tubes) that carry blood. Here oxygen, in the alveloi, passes into the blood so it can be transported around the body.

At the same time waste-rich blood releases its carbon dioxide into the alveoli. It takes the opposite journey out of the body; exhaled air contains an increased amount of carbon dioxide. The whole process is called gaseous exchange.

To summarise, the respiratory system has two main functions:

1. to bring oxygen into the body

2. to take carbon dioxide out of the body.

A lot of oxygen is breathed out as well as in. This is why expired air resuscitation (EAR) is given by mouth when someone has stopped breathing, for example after drowning. Inhaled air contains 20 per cent oxygen and 0.04 per cent carbon dioxide; exhaled air contains 16 per cent oxygen and 4 per cent carbon dioxide.

The body needs less oxygen at rest because the muscles are not working so hard, and more when they are working hard e.g. running a 400m race. An average person breathes about 21 times a minute during rest. More air is taken in with each breath during exercise as more oxygen is required to give the muscles energy. Vigorous exercise may result in breathing more deeply or panting, but there should be no wheezing or bubbling sounds such as might occur during a cold or flu. Regular exercise increases lung capacity and enables more oxygen to be taken in with each breath.

edexcel ▦ examiner tip
You will not be tested upon your understanding of how the respiratory system works but it will help you understand other parts of this topic.

Tidal volume and vital capacity

These two measurements help to estimate the efficiency of the respiratory system. It is important to be able to define tidal volume and vital capacity.

- **Tidal volume** is the amount of air inspired and expired with each normal breath at rest or during exercise.

- **Vital capacity** is the greatest amount of air that can be made to pass into and out of the lungs by the most forceful inspiration and expiration. Normally this is about 4 to 5 litres.

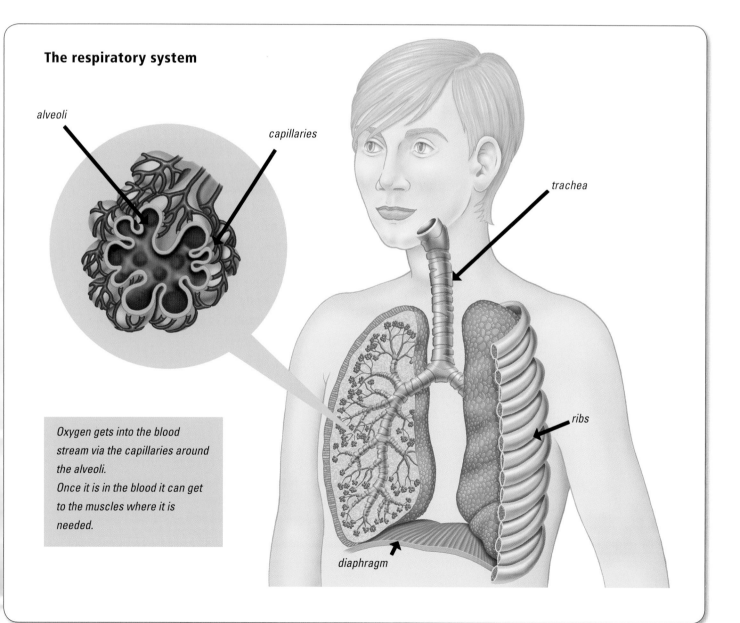

The respiratory system

alveoli

capillaries

trachea

ribs

diaphragm

Oxygen gets into the blood stream via the capillaries around the alveoli.
Once it is in the blood it can get to the muscles where it is needed.

28: Immediate and long-term effects of exercise on the respiratory system

Objectives

At the end of this chapter you should know:

- the immediate effects of participation in exercise
- the long-term effects of regular participation in exercise
- the effects of smoking on the respiratory system.

It is very important to remember that an efficient respiratory system aids the cardiovascular system by providing a constant supply of oxygen for the muscles and by removing carbon dioxide. This is why efficient cardiovascular and respiratory systems (cardio-respiratory systems) are so important to everyone, not just elite sports stars, and are vital to both health and performance in sport and physical activity.

edexcel ::: key terms

Oxygen debt: the extra oxygen consumed during recovery from a period of strenuous physical activity, compared with the amount which would usually have been consumed over the same length of time at rest.

Immediate and short-term effects of participation in exercise and physical activity on the respiratory system

During exercise or while taking part in a strenuous sport, several changes take place in the body:

Breathing quickens and deepens

Breathing is greatly affected by exercise. However quickly the heart beats, it cannot carry enough oxygen if not enough is reaching the lungs. The efficiency of breathing depends on how much oxygen can be removed from the air The most important structures in oxygen uptake are the alveoli, and these can be damaged, for example by smoking.

Oxygen debt

Strenuous exercise may result in a need for more oxygen than can be supplied through breathing. Oxygen used during anaerobic exercise often results in oxygen debt and is repaid through deep gasping breaths at the end of the activity. These enable as much oxygen as possible to be taken into the respiratory system, while eliminating as much as possible of the waste produced, mainly in the form of carbon dioxide. This may occur, for example, at the end of a long race such as the 400m race when the best runners complete in around 45 seconds and are very out of breath.

ResultsPlus
Build Better Answers

(i) **During a match a player is likely to build up an oxygen debt. What is an oxygen debt? (1)**

(ii) **If a player has built up an oxygen debt will she have been working aerobically or anaerobically? (1)**

(iii) **What by-product is associated with an oxygen debt? (1)**

Answer: (i) A lack of oxygen

(ii) Anaerobically

(iii) Lactic acid

Examiner's tip: Although questions are mostly on one topic alone, in some cases you may find knowledge of more than one topic is needed. Being able to apply your knowledge in this was will help you to get top marks.

Students often struggle with questions on oxygen debt. Make sure you practice questions on this to test your knowledge.

Effects of regular participation in and long-term benefits of exercise and physical activity

After a sustained period of regular participation the improved efficiency of the lungs will allow better delivery of oxygen to the working muscles, which means that the body will be able to cope better during exercise. Carbon dioxide is removed more efficiently, which means that the body can cope with a greater increase in the production of carbon dioxide during exercise. Vital capacity is increased as the whole system, particularly the lungs, becomes more efficient.

More alveoli become available for gaseous exchange after regular exercise, which means more oxygen can be absorbed by the capillaries and more carbon dioxide taken from them. As a result VO2 max (aerobic capacity) is increased. Furthermore as we have seen in topic 1.2.2 regular exercise also increases the number of blood vessels. The increase in capillaries around the alveoli means more oxygen can get into the blood and through the muscles.

The effects of smoking on the alveoli and gaseous exchange

Taking oxygen into the body and expelling carbon dioxide through gaseous exchange are the vital requirements of the respiratory system. Smoking can have serious adverse affects on this process. Smoke damages the lungs and especially the alveoli, making them less stretchy and so less efficient. As a result, it becomes more difficult to get oxygen in and carbon dioxide out, and smokers may become short of breath. Their hearts have to work harder to get the oxygen their bodies need and consequently they feel tired. The ban on smoking in public places is one way in which the government is attempting to tackle this problem.

Apply it!

Devise a way to measure your breathing rate. Measure your breathing rate. Then undertake some short fast exercise and record your breathing rate again. Compare the two scores with those of your colleagues.

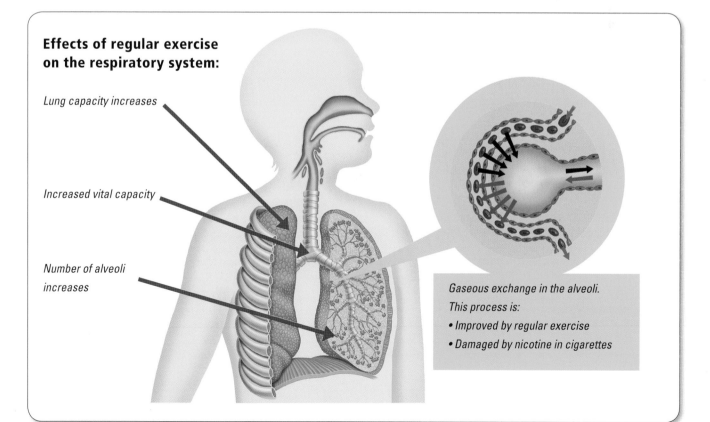

Effects of regular exercise on the respiratory system:

Lung capacity increases

Increased vital capacity

Number of alveoli increases

Gaseous exchange in the alveoli. This process is:
- *Improved by regular exercise*
- *Damaged by nicotine in cigarettes*

examzone

Know Zone
Topic 1.2.3: A healthy, active lifestyle and your respiratory system

In this topic you will learn how your lifestyle affects your respiratory system, what happens when you are actually exercising, and the effects of exercising over a short period of time, for example when performing your 6-week PEP and on a regular basis over a long period of time.

You should know...

☐ The immediate and short-term effects of participation in exercise and physical activity.

☐ The long-term effects of regular participation in exercise and physical activity.

☐ The need for rest and recovery time.

☐ The effects of recreational drugs on the respiratory system.

Examiner's tip

Know the terms 'tidal volume', 'vital capacity' and 'oxygen debt'. Revise what they mean, how to explain them, and how they are affected by exercise during and following a PEP.

Key terms

Tidal volume
Vital capacity
Oxygen debt

Stretch activity

If you have experienced oxygen debt you will have felt a build up of lactic acid in the muscles (see topic 1.2.4 also) and you should know that this happens when you work anaerobically. See topic 1.1.4 for more on anaerobic exercise which can lead to oxygen debt.

Support activity

You could take photographs while you are exercising and put them into your PEP. An example might be you out of breath and breathing deeply (an immediate effect of exercise), or experiencing oxygen debt after an interval or circuit training session. The photograph will indicate an immediate effect of exercise which you should be able to explain. At the same time, you should note tidal volume and vital capacity.

Question: Name the term described in each of the following statements.
The amount of air breathed in or out of the lungs in one breath. (1)
The maximum amount of air that can be forcibly exhaled after breathing in as much as possible. (1)
The amount of oxygen consumed during recovery above that which would have been ordinarily been consumed in the same time at rest. (1)

Students' answer	Examiners' comments	Build Better Answers
a) stroke volume	Incorrect answer. Some candidates made no attempt to answer the question or got mixed up with the heart.	Tidal volume
b) Vo2 max	Vo2 max is wrong, and it is not part of the specification. Vo2 max actually refers to the amount of oxygen one can use.	Vital capacity
c) cardiac output	Incorrect answer. Again, the student refers to a key term relating to the cardiovascular system: a clear mistake.	Oxygen debt

A lot of students struggled with these questions, just like this example. More than 50% of candidates got 0/1 on each part of this question. These are all points that you can and do experience when you exercise, especially oxygen debt, but still only 35% of students got a mark for this. You should also be able to explain them if you are given the term.

For the most part these are questions where you either know or do not know the answer; you cannot work them out so you have to learn them. It will help if you test yourself on all the key terms in this topic.

Practice Exam Questions

1. (i) During a match a player builds up an oxygen debt. What is an oxygen debt? (1)

   (ii) If a player has built up an oxygen debt will she have been working aerobically or anaerobically? (1)

   (iii) What by-product is associated with an oxygen debt? (1)

   (iv) State TWO ways in which the performer could help to remove this by-product. (2)

2. An increase in breathing rate is an example of:

   a long-term benefit of exercise

   a poor level of fitness

   an immediate effect of exercise

   an effect of regular training. (1)

138

Muscles and movement

Muscles are attached to the bones of the skeleton by tendons. Each muscle is made of many cells or muscle fibres. When muscle fibres contract, or pull against the skeleton, movement takes place. What they cannot do is push. Most voluntary muscles are long and thin, but when they contract they get shorter and thicker.

When a muscle is contracted it pulls on a bone, often producing movement in one direction at a joint. However, because muscles cannot push, the joint also needs to be able to allow the bone to move in the opposite direction. This is achieved by a second muscle that pulls the bone the other way.

Muscles are arranged in **antagonistic pairs**, so when one muscle contracts and pulls the other relaxes to allow the joint to work. The biceps and triceps muscles in the upper arm are arranged in this way so that the elbow joint can be bent (flexed) and straightened (extended). This pair of muscles works antagonistically during a bicep curl or tricep dip.

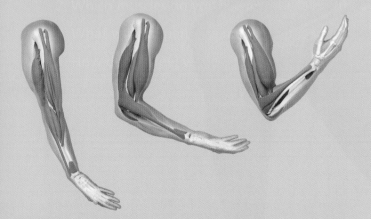

The same actions take place in the leg around the knee joint with the quadriceps and the hamstring working **antagonistically**. When the quadriceps contracts the hamstring relaxes and the leg straightens. This pair of muscles works like this during such exercises as a leg press and squats.

The muscles

There are 11 (the number of players in a football team) specific muscles you need to know for the examination. Starting from the top of the body and working downwards they are:

1. deltoid
2. trapezius
3. latissimus dorsi
4. pectorals
5. abdominals
6. biceps
7. triceps
8. gluteals
9. quadriceps
10. hamstrings
11. gastrocnemius.

Apply it!

Task 1. Contract your biceps and see what happens. Now try contracting your biceps and triceps at the same time. You will see that no movement takes place because both muscles were contracted and neither was relaxed.

Task 2. Can you draw two diagrams showing the antagonistic muscle pair working at the knee joint to move the tibia and fibia (the lower leg bones)?

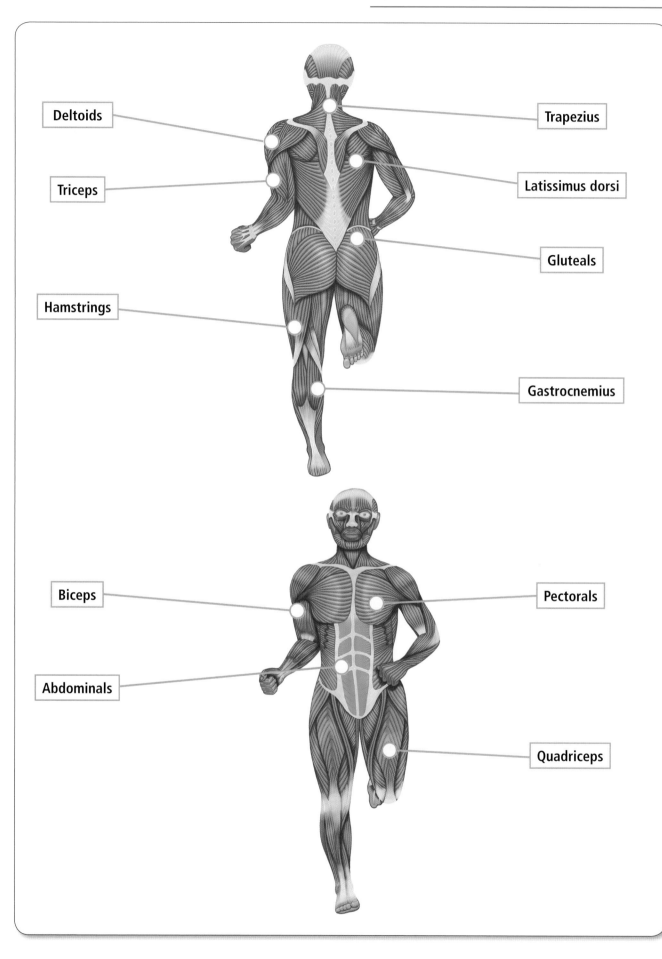

Deltoids

Trapezius

Triceps

Latissimus dorsi

Gluteals

Hamstrings

Gastrocnemius

Biceps

Pectorals

Abdominals

Quadriceps

The deltoid
The deltoid gives the rounded shape to the shoulder. It is a powerful muscle that abducts (takes away) the upper arm from the body. The deltoid is mainly responsible for lifting the arm above the head, for example, serving in tennis. Its strength can be improved by exercises such as bent over rowing and military press.

The trapezius
The trapezius is attached to the head and neck at the top, and the shoulder below. Its function is to lift the shoulder, brace it back, and rotate the scapula (shoulder blade). If a person has drooping shoulders it may indicate a weak trapezius. This muscle can be developed by performing rowing and shoulder shrugs as part of a weight training programme.

The lattisimus dorsi
Lattisimus dorsi is a broad sheet of muscle which extends from the lower region of the spine to the humerus (the bone in the upper arm). It is a powerful muscle which abducts the arms (brings them toward from the body) and rotates, to draws them back and inwards towards the body. It can be developed by performing lat pull-downs on the weights machine, or pull-ups.

The pectoral muscle
The pectoral muscle covers the chest. This is another powerful muscle which works to adduct the arm (move it towards the body) and draw the arm forwards to rotate it inwards. This muscle is important in the swimming strokes front crawl and butterfly. The bench press is a good exercise to improve its strength.

The abdominal muscles
These hold the stomach in. They make flexing, bending forward and rotating the trunk to the side possible, and also help good posture. These muscles can be strengthened by performing sit-ups correctly, but crunches give just as good a result and place much less stress on the back. Many other exercises also help to develop the abdominals; most do not require any weights or machines.

Rowing is one example of an activity that uses the abdominal muscles.

The biceps and triceps

These muscles are described together because that is how they work – together. The biceps is probably the best known muscle in the body, and it is found at the front of the upper arm. The tricep is found at the back of the upper arm. When the arm is straightened (extended), the triceps contracts while the biceps relaxes. The biceps and triceps are involved with throwing actions, such as throwing the javelin or a cricket ball.

Many exercises can be used to strengthen the biceps, but the most popular are either barbell or dumbbell curls, or preacher curls. The triceps stretch (extension) can be used to strengthen the triceps. Chin-ups, parallel bar dips, and press-ups improve the strength of both these muscles and are also good tests of their fitness and strength.

The gluteal muscles

These form the buttocks. As its name implies, the largest of the gluteal muscles is the gluteus maximus. It lies just beneath the skin and is attached to the femur (the thigh bone – the largest bone in the body). Its function is to pull the leg backwards (extension). The gluteus maximus is another muscle which could cause poor posture if under-developed. Many weight-training exercises help to develop this muscle, including squats, leg press, and lunges.

The gluteal muscles can also be strengthened without weights by kneeling on the floor or a yoga mat and extending the right leg backwards and left arm forwards, then reversing the exercise by extending the left leg backwards and the right arm forwards, at the same time keeping the body in line.

The quadriceps

The quadriceps are found on the front of the upper leg. As the name implies, there are four of them. The knee joint is tested for reactions by tapping the patella (knee-cap) tendon which joins the quadriceps to the patella. The quadriceps extend (extension) or straighten the leg at the knee joint. Their most common sporting use is when kicking a ball, which is why they are sometimes known as the kicking muscles. Many exercises are suitable for strengthening them, including squats, seated leg press, legs extensions

142

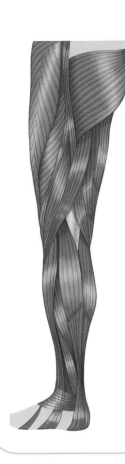

The hamstrings

The hamstrings are found on the back of the leg and stretch from the bottom part of the pelvis to the tibia (the shin bone); they are so close to the surface that they can be felt behind the knee. They bend (flex) the knee and its tendons. The hamstrings are of great importance in running, and are sometimes referred to as the 'sprinter's muscle'. It is most important to warm them up properly before sprinting as this activity can often cause them to be injured. Leg curls are a popular exercise to increase their strength, but as they are not as strong as the quadriceps a lighter weight is used.

The gastrocnemius

The gastrocnemius (and soleus) are the muscles which form most of what is commonly called the calf muscle. The gastrocnemius starts at the back of the femur and the soleus at the back of the tibia and fibula. They come together to form the Achilles tendon, which can be seen at the back of the ankle. The function of these muscles is to point the toes (plantar flex) away from the foot, which results in a slight spring in the step.

The leg muscles are the largest and strongest in the body, and are obviously very important in most physical activities. In sports such as tennis, golf, and especially throwing events in athletics, the initial movement comes from the legs and is finished in the upper body. Inefficient use of the powerful muscles in the lower body is often the cause of poor performance in these activities.

edexcel ⋮⋮⋮ examiner tip

Do not use abbreviations such as pecs for pectorals, abs for abdominal, glutes for gluteals or quads for quadriceps.

Apply it!

Draw a table with eight columns. In the left hand column list the muscles described here. Use the words below as column headings. Add ticks to the columns to show the movements that can be created by each muscle.
Flexion, extension, adduction, abduction, rotation, plantar flexion, dorsi flexion.

e.g. biceps = flexion

Summary table		
Muscle	**produces**	**example**
Deltoid	Abducts the upper arm, from the body	Serve in tennis
Trapezius	Rotates the shoulder blades backwards	Rowing
Lattisimus dorsi	Rotates upper arm at the shoulders	Swimming butterfly
Pectoral muscle	Adduction of arm	Swimming front crawl
Abdominal muscles	Flexion and rotation of trunk	Rowing
Biceps	Flexion of arm at the elbow	Bending the arm to throw a cricket ball
Triceps	Extension of arm at the elbow	Straightening the arm to throw a cricket ball
Gluteus maximus	Extension of the upper leg	Running and for maintaining good posture
Quadriceps	Extension of the leg at the knee	Kicking a football
Hamstrings	Flexion of the leg at the knee	Sprinting: when leg bends
Gastrocnemius	Plantar flexion of the foot	Running: pushing onto the toes

30: Exercising the muscular system

Objectives

By the end of this chapter you should understand:

- the immediate impact of physical activity and exercise on your muscular system
- the effects of regular participation in exercise and physical activity
- the potential for injuries such as muscle strain and muscle atrophy and their treatment using common techniques.

LINK IT UP!

To look back at how the increased demand for oxygen from the muscles is managed by the respiratory system go to CH 27. To revise the build up of lactic acid see CH 24.

edexcel ⠿ key terms

Isometric contractions: Muscle contraction which results in increased tension but the length does not alter, for example when pressing against a stationary object.

Isotonic contraction: Muscle contraction that results in limb movement.

The immediate effects of exercise on the muscular system

Exercise increases the body's demand for oxygen and glycogen as the muscles need more fuel to function: contracting and lengthening at an increased rate. Extra waste products are created when muscles work harder than normal, and extra blood needs to be pumped around the body to take these waste products away. It is possible to continue exercising aerobically for a long time as long as the intensity is not too high, but when the demand **for oxygen** is so high that not enough can be provided to the muscles, **lactic acid** begins to build up until eventually it is not possible to continue. This is because lactic acid makes muscles ache and can cause **cramp**. Regular exercise and training can help the muscles cope better with these demands.

How muscles work

To move, or exercise, muscles must contract and lengthen. There are two types of contraction:

Isotonic contractions

Muscles can pull but they cannot push, so they must work in pairs to create movement: one works while the other relaxes. This is called an isotonic contraction and occurs when a muscle contracts and works over a range of movement. For example, when performing a press-up, the biceps muscle (at the front of the upper arm) contracts to bend the arm at the elbow, lowering the body in a controlled way. While this is happening, the triceps (the muscle at the back of the upper arm) relaxes. When the body is raised, the triceps contracts, straightening the arm, and the biceps relaxes. When muscles work in this way they are said to be antagonistic.

There are many examples of isotonic muscle action; the most obvious are perhaps walking and running. The hamstring (the muscle at the back of the thigh) contracts as the leg is lifted. When the leg is lowered, the hamstring lengthens and relaxes and the quadriceps (muscle at the front of the thigh) contracts. Imagine how many times these muscles will go through this process in a marathon! Most weight and circuit training exercises use isotonic contractions.

144

Apply it!

Think of two other examples of isometric muscle contractions in sport or physical activity.

Isometric contractions

Isometric contractions occur when the muscle contracts but stays in a fixed position. One example of this is the plank position (a yoga position), where the press-up is held in the straight arm position so the muscle is working (contracting) without movement taking place. Another isometric contraction could be at the opposite end of the press-up, where the position is held with arms bent and chin very near the floor. In yoga, this is known as the stick position (see photograph below.)

Isometric contractions are not used during sport as much as isotonic contractions, but they are used on occasion, for example in a rugby scrum.

LINK IT UP!

For more information about muscular strength and muscular endurance go to CH8.

Apply it!

Try to perform 10 press-ups. Hold the plank position for 30 seconds. Then try to hold the stick position for 30 seconds. Think about your muscles contracting in these exercises.

Choosing a personal exercise programme

The programme you choose to follow will depend upon personal circumstances; for example, your age, what you want to achieve, your event or activity, and probably the time you have available to train. It is important to know which muscle groups you are going to work on so you know which exercises to use. For most people a core programme working on the upper body, abdominal muscles, and lower body would be suitable.

Long-term effects of participation in exercise and physical activity

The whole muscular system benefits from regular exercise. This includes the involuntary muscles (often referred to as smooth muscles) and the voluntary muscles (also known as skeletal muscles). The skeletal muscles contract to provide movement and are important to stability and posture. As muscles grow in strength as a result of regular training, they also increase in size.

Increased muscle size – hypertrophy

Training using the principle of progressive overload, for example with weights, applies varying levels of stress to the skeletal muscles. This results in them being damaged as the tiny muscle fibres are pulled apart causing trauma. The human body is very clever and when it rebuilds the bridges between the muscle fibres – a complicated process which may take up to 48 hours – it actually makes itself slightly stronger. This is one of the reasons why allowing time for rest and recovery is so important. The resulting increase in muscle mass is known as muscle hypertrophy. It also leads to an increase in strength. The many other long-term effects and benefits of increased muscle mass include improved muscular strength and endurance. With increased strength comes increased power (strength x speed). This produces a firmer looking body, better posture, and stronger tendons (which join muscles to bones), and ligaments (which join bones to bones). The bones also increase in strength. These positive effects also lower the risk of injury in these areas.

Potential injuries to the muscular system

Strength training either through exercise or a training programme helps to develop muscles and results in the benefits described above. However, stopping strength training results in loss of muscle mass and strength. This is known as **muscle atrophy**, and can be a problem for sportspeople. Often when sportspeople are injured they experience muscle atrophy.

Soft tissue injuries to muscles

The most common injuries to muscles include tears, pulls, and strains. These terms often describe similar types of injury: the small muscle fibres may be torn from their attachment to a tendon. These fibres shorten when the muscle contracts and relax when it is used antagonistically. During intense competition the muscle fibres contract and relax very quickly, and this can cause the connective tissue and the blood vessels which run inside them to be torn.

Many sportspeople, especially footballers, have strong, very well-developed quadriceps (the kicking muscle in front of the thigh) because the nature of invasion games is that these muscles get plenty of exercise. Hamstrings, the tendons at the back of the leg, are often pulled and for this reason need special attention when warming up. This part of an exercise session can greatly reduce the chance of injury.

Warm-up

Warming up before any exercise session or competition is crucial to minimise the potential for injury. A warm-up session begins by raising the heart rate and warming up the muscles with some gentle and progressively more energetic exercise, such as jogging. This is followed by some exercises and stretching, which should be specific to the main activity. For example, sprinters or footballers would do hamstring and quadriceps stretches respectively, followed by strides and short sprints.

edexcel ::: examiner tip
Remember! You strain a muscle and sprain a joint.

Cool-down

The aim of cooling down after any activity is to bring the heart rate gradually back to normal, and to disperse any lactic acid from the muscles so that they do not become stiff and sore. Cooling down properly also ensures readiness for the next exercise session or game. Stretches are included in the cool-down, and should be held for 20 to 30 seconds.

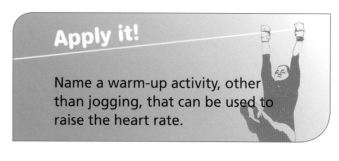

Apply it!

Name a warm-up activity, other than jogging, that can be used to raise the heart rate.

Treatment for muscular injuries

RICE treatment is used for muscle strains. If a player injures a muscle during a professional game, physiotherapists will usually be available to give the RICE treatment. The player stops playing to rest the injury and will continue to rest it if necessary. The first 24 to 48 hours are crucial with this type of injury and the player should continue to rest during this time.

Muscle injuries can prevent a person from training and this inactivity can cause **muscle atrophy**.

LINK IT UP!

To learn about RICE treatment go to Topic 1.2.5 CH 35.

31: Lifestyle, performance-enhancing drugs and the muscular system

146

Objectives

By the end of this chapter you should understand how the muscular system is affected by:

○ rest

○ diet

○ performance-enhancing drugs, such as steroids.

Rest

Rest allows muscles to repair the damage caused by exercise, rebuild before the next exercise session, and strengthen. As described earlier, this is how muscles develop. This is one of the reasons why rest and recovery need to be built into any personal exercise programme.

In a personal exercise programme, planned rest is short-term recovery. Long-term recovery should also be built into a long-term exercise programme, such as a one-year preparation for competition. Athletes preparing for high level competition in this way taper or reduce their programme by cutting down on the number of training sessions each week but increase the intensity of each session. Once the competition is over, they take a complete break from training before starting again to prepare for the next season or competition. Recreational athletes should use the same model to develop their long-term programmes, as too much training and too little rest can lead to over-training.

LINK IT UP!

To remind yourself about rest as a principle of training go to CH 11.
Or, if you want to see how rest enhances the cardiovascular system go to CH 26.

Diet

Proper nutrition is another important part of the recovery process. Energy stores need to be replenished soon after exercise, with carbohydrates and fluids (energy drinks and water). For the muscular system to recover it is essential to have adequate amounts of protein in a diet, as it helps muscles to be repaired and rebuilt, preventing atrophy. As a result protein is important for any sportsperson, such as a rugby player or weightlifter, who needs to build and maintain muscle. It is also important to eat within two hours of stopping exercise; eating after a longer interval is not as beneficial.

Performance enhancing drugs

The best way to build and repair muscles is through safe and effective training methods backed up by a balanced diet. Some athletes also use supplements, such as protein pills. But this is not necessary if the athlete eats a proper balanced diet.

Some sportspeople also use banned substances called performance-enhancing drugs. Anabolic steroids are the most common form of these. They are used to build muscle both in size, which is why some body builders may use them, and strength, which is why athletes such as sprinters and throwers may be tempted to use them. They increase size and strength quickly, and also speed up the recovery process after training. As a result, athletes who use them can train harder and more often. They can also help athletes to recover more quickly from injury. Performance enhancing drugs give the people who take them an unfair advantage, which is one reason why they are banned. For example, British sprinter Dwain Chambers was banned from athletes for two years after testing positive for a performance enhancing drug, and the American Olympic sprint champion Marion Jones had to return all her Olympic gold medals. An even more important reason not to take these drugs is that they can seriously damage your health.

LINK IT UP!

In CH 22, you will learn about the categories of drugs and how others affect the body.

How does a strong muscular system help in everyday life?

Strength is necessary in everyday life to:

1. increase work capacity

2. decrease the chance of injury

3. prevent low back pain – a common problem

4. improve or prevent poor posture – a common problem

5. improve athletic performance

6. aid rehabilitation after illness or injury.

Apply it!

Write down three ways in which increased strength would benefit you in your daily life.

Builders need a strong muscular system to do their job and help prevent injuries.

ResultsPlus
Exam Question Report

(i) Name the muscle responsible for bending the arm at the elbow joint. (1)
After a tennis player strikes the ball, the racket arm will follow through so that it moves across the body.
(ii) Name the muscle responsible for adducting the upper arm at the shoulder. (1)
(June 2008, 2 marks)

Answer

Biceps/biceps brachii

Pectoralis major/pectorals (Pecs was not accepted)

How students answered part (i)

As biceps and triceps are commonly used together, some students mistakenly put triceps. Students must be sure of which muscle is used to flex the arm at the elbow (bicep) and which is used for extending it.

| | 30% | 0 marks |

The muscle for bending the arm was well known. The bicep is the muscle most students are familiar with.

| | 70% | 1 mark |

How students answered part (ii)

Candidates found the final section of this question very difficult. A variety of answers were given ranging from the trapesius to triceps although some candidates correctly stated the pectorals.

| | 86% | 0 marks |

Only 14% of students knew the answer for this. They will have known what adduction meant and have been familiar with the muscles. Also, they wouldn't have used 'pecs'.

| | 14% | 1 mark |

examzone

Know Zone
Topic 1.2.4: A healthy, active lifestyle and your muscular system

In this topic you will learn how your lifestyle affects your muscular system, what happens when you are actually exercising, and the effects of exercising over a short period of time, for example when performing your 6-week PEP, and on a regular basis over a long period of time. You will also learn how to build up the muscles (hypertrophy) and what will happen if you stop training or are injured (muscle atrophy).

You should know...

- [ ] The major muscle groups and which physical activities benefit them.
- [ ] The role of muscles in movement.
- [ ] The immediate and short-term effects of participation in exercise and physical activity on the muscular system.
- [ ] The effects of regular participation in – and long-term effects of participation in – exercise and physical activity on the muscular system.
- [ ] The potential for injuries such as muscle strain and muscle atrophy and their treatment using common techniques.
- [ ] The need for rest.
- [ ] The effects of diet.
- [ ] The effects of performance enhancing drugs, such as steroids.

Key terms

RICE

Isometric contraction   Hypertrophy

Isotonic contraction   Muscle atrophy

Anabolic steroids.

Stretch activity

Make notes in your PEP on the muscles you worked and why and how you included rest and recovery. Are you including more protein in your diet to help build and repair muscle while doing your PEP? You could also include some information about performance-enhancing drugs and why people take them; about muscle hypertrophy; and about the principle of reversibility which causes muscle atrophy.

Support activity

Ask someone to take photographs during your circuit and weight training sessions or even your warm up which show you exercising and working on the various muscle groups, and demonstrate different types of muscle contraction. If you are doing exercise activities you can use this knowledge to expand and improve your PEP, demonstrating your knowledge as a fitness instructor and informed exerciser.

Examiner's tip

There is a lot to learn in this topic; you need to know the names of muscles, what actions they cause and in what sporting actions they are used. You can learn and apply much of this while you are performing your PEP. Make sure you write it into your PEP so that you can revise it later and be able to apply it if required to do so in examination questions.

ResultsPlus
Maximise your marks

Question:
(a) The muscles in a gymnast's body work to maintain an upright, stationary position.
What type of muscle contraction is taking place? (1)

(b) Name and explain another type of muscle contraction and give an example of its use in sport.
(i) Name of contraction _____ (1)
(ii) Explanation _____ (1)
(iii) Example of its use in sport _____ (1)

Students' answer	Examiners' comments	Build Better Answers
a) Isometric	▲ Correct	
b) (i) Isotonic	▲ Correct. Learn these two terms from your practical performance, for example the difference between plank position (isometric) and press ups (isotonic).	
(ii) Where the muscles work together, one relaxes and the other contracts.	■ This is not an explanation of isotonic but an explanation of antagonistic. This student knows the terms but doesn't understand them.	This is when a muscle contracts and movement takes place e.g. in the legs and the arms.
(iii) It can be used in dumb-bell curling. When the weight moves towards you the tricep contracts and the bicep relaxes and when it goes the other way, from you, the bicep contracts and the tricep relaxes.	● This answer is not acceptable as the student is describing antagonistic movement following on from their answer to (ii) above.	An example would be when walking, running or jumping in athletics or kicking a football.

More than 50% of students failed to get a mark for 1 of these 4 questions. 79% failed to get a mark when asked to explain an isotonic contraction, when all they needed to write was: this is when muscles contract and movement takes place.

You should have experienced both isometric and isotonic contractions at various points in the practical course as well as learning it in the theory lessons. If you did circuit training you will have performed bench dips and could have experienced both in this exercise as well as in the press up and plank positions. If you have a photograph of yourself doing the actions and build this into your PEP it should stay with you for longer and you will be more likely to recall it and explain it in the examination.

Practice Exam Questions

1 Exercises can be isotonic or isometric. Explain the terms.
Isotonic (1)   Isometric (1)

2 As a badminton player stretches to reach a shuttlecock she has to stop suddenly due to a great pain in her hamstrings. What type of injury is she likely to have sustained? (1)

3 Sprinters suffer from muscle injuries. A balanced diet can help recovery after injury. What food group aids growth and repair of tissues? (1)

Topic 1.2.5: A healthy, active lifestyle and your skeletal system

Sport in Context

Danny Cipriani, the England rugby player, is involved in one of the most physically punishing sports. His skeleton is essential for his safety when he plays: during a tackle, his rib cage protects his vital organs. His muscles pull and move his bones when he kicks and runs.

In this topic you will learn about the skeletal system, the effects of regular exercise on the bones, ligaments and tendons of the body, and the importance of a good diet. You will also learn about the importance of weight bearing exercise, such as walking and running, and its significance regarding bone density and the prevention of osteoporosis. You will look at the many potential injuries to bones and joints and their treatment.

PE and me

1. What do you think is the most important function of the skeleton? Why?

2. What is a joint?

3. What are the different types of movement that can occur at the joints?

4. Can you think of injuries that might happen to the bones and joints when taking part in sport?

Topic Overview

By the end of this topic you will be able to:

● describe the functions of the skeletal system

● explain the movement possibilities at joints

● understand how regular exercise benefits the skeletal system.

32: The skeletal system

Objectives

At the end of this chapter you will understand the three functions of the skeletal system during physical activity.

What is the skeletal system and what does it do?

The skeletal system includes all the bones in the body, from the cranium (skull) to the bones that make up the foot. It maintains the body's shape and supports it, keeps it in position, and provides a structure to which the muscles are attached. It has three main functions:

1. movement

2. support

3. protection

The function of the skeleton

1. Movement

Where bones meet they form joints, which act as levers. Tendons attach the bones to muscles, enabling a variety of movements both fine (such as threading a needle with cotton) and coarse (such as throwing a hammer in athletics).

2. Support

The skeleton supports the body in a variety of positions – standing up, sitting, lying down. It can also support other, more complicated positions. Tom Daly, for example, does a handstand before taking off for some of his dives. The bones and skeletal system give the body shape. The skeleton acts as a framework for the body and also affects body composition and frame size.

3. Protection

Another function of the skeleton is **protection**. The cranium (skull) protects the brain. The spine, or vertebral column, protects the spinal chord. The ribs which form the chest protect the heart and lungs, some abdominal organs such as the liver and spleen, and to some extent the stomach and kidneys. Petr Cech, a goalkeeper, had his skull damaged during a football match. His cranium prevented a severe injury to his brain.

ResultsPlus
Exam Question Report

One function of the skeleton is to enable movement.
(i)   State another function of the skeleton. (1)
(ii)   Give an example of the use of this function when participating in physical activity. (1)
(June 2006, 2 marks)

Answer

(i)   Function   protection; support

(ii) Example   cranium protects the brain; gives us upright posture for running (or equivalent)

Note 1: check example matches function
Note 2: must demonstrate physical activity context

How Students answered part (i)

Some students that got this wrong referred to movement. The question specifically asks for 'another' function.

| 17% | 0 marks |

Many candidates were aware of the main functions of the skeleton. The popular answer was 'protection', which was then relatively easy for the candidate to apply in part (ii).

| 83% | 1 mark |

How Students answered part (ii)

Most students failed to get the mark here because they couldn't apply their knowledge. The students who put an incorrect function of the skeleton in part (i) will also have failed to get a mark.

| 76% | 0 marks |

The students who were able to get this right applied their knowledge by giving examples, and putting it in context. There were some good examples of application of protection, often focusing on rugby tackles (cranium protecting the brain; ribs protecting the heart/lungs); or boxing and blows to the body.

| 24% | 1 mark |

The functions of the skeletal system in practice

Diver Tom Daly is a good example of how all these functions work together.

In his dive from the 10 metres board, he uses energy climbing the steps to the diving platform as well as diving. As described in topic 1.2.2, this energy is transported in his blood in the form of glycogen, so blood production is vital. **Movement** takes place throughout the preparation (getting up the steps to the diving platform) and execution of the dive. For example, Tom Daly starts in a standing position but may have to take up a handstand position before diving. At this point he is **supported** upside down and balanced in the handstand position by his arms.

He changes shape several times in a split second, going through a range of coordinated movements (somersaults and twists) at great speed using his agility and reaction time to complete the dive successfully. As he hits the water, his cranium **protects** his head, his ribs his heart and lungs and other vital organs.

Tom's event is a highly technical one and a fit body has helped him to achieve success at a very young age. The way his body functions, combined with his highly developed skills, enables him to perform at this level.

33: Joints and movement

154

Objectives

At the end of this chapter you should know:

○ the ranges of movment possible at a hinge and ball and socket joint (flexion, extension, abduction, adduction and rotation)

The structure of joints

A joint is a place where two or more bones meet. If our bodies were not jointed we would be very awkward and clumsy, and our activities would be extremely restricted.

In order to prevent pain through the friction which might be caused by the bones rubbing together, the ends of the bones in a synovial joint are covered with a layer of thick cartilage, known as hyaline cartilage. The cartilage is made up of a group of cells which are surrounded by fluid. The cartilage is elastic and this enables it to cushion and therefore protect the ends of the bones involved in the joint. Surrounding a joint is a tough capsule, which produces synovial fluid to lubricate the joint.

Joints allow movement. For instance, the spine is made up of a number of small bones which allow the back to be flexible; a characteristic that allows high jumpers to bend over a bar. Generally speaking, the joints in the upper limbs allow mobility (for example, bringing food to the mouth) and joints in the lower limbs are for stability: maintaining the body's small base – a person would easily fall over if the muscles were not constantly moving the joints to adjust balance.

Jointed bones and flexible fingers allow people to do things that few other animals are capable of doing.

For example, people (along with some monkeys and apes) have opposable thumbs, which means that the thumb can be pressed to the other fingers to form a pincer movement. This is possible because there is a special type of joint between the first metacarpal bone and the one next to it.

Movement at joints

All joints allow movement but the extent and freedom varies from joint to joint. In GCSE PE we are concerned with flexion, extension, adduction, abduction and rotation.

Hinge joints

The elbow joint

The elbow is a hinge joint. It allows the arm to bend (flex), or straighten (extend), as happens when doing curls in the weights room or bench dips in circuit training. The most common example of flexion and extension of the elbow joint is bending the arm when eating. The muscles which flex the joint are on the front of the arm (biceps), and the muscles which extend it are on the back (triceps).

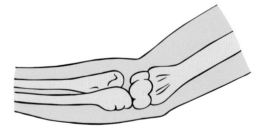

The knee joint

This is the largest and most complex joint. The tibia (shin bone) is hinged on the femur (thigh bone) so that the leg can be bent (flexed) or straightened (extended), such as when a footballer bends the lower leg at the knee preparing to kick the ball (flexion) and then straightens it to strike the ball (extension). Squats or seated leg presses are another good example, although perhaps the sergeant jump is the best. Flexing the knee joint is similar to swinging a pendulum. It requires minimal effort at the joint, and this prevents it from wearing out too soon.

This joint can also be rotated slightly. The knee joint is an articulation of the condyles (the rounded ends) of the femur (thigh bone) and the tibia (shin bone). Unlike the shoulder and the hip, there is no socket at the knee (or the elbow), just two smooth shallow surfaces which are in contact. Two short but very strong ligaments, about the thickness of a little finger, prevent the bones from sliding apart. These are called the cruciate ligaments and they tie the bones together very efficiently by crossing inside the joint. Footballers often damage these ligaments in hard tackles. The resulting injury is often severe and can in some cases end a player's career.

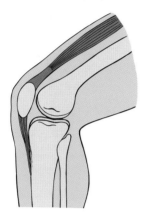

Inside the joint are semi-lunar cartilages on the condyles of the tibia (shin bone); these are for lubrication rather than stability. Sportspeople often have 'cartilage trouble', which happens when the cartilage is torn, often following a sudden twist of the knee. The knee is put under greater strain than any other joint in the body, and it is not uncommon for sportspeople to play until their knees can no longer hold out! As a result of this strain, the knee produces more synovial fluid than the other synovial joints.

Ball and socket joints
The shoulder and hip joints
These are called ball and socket joints because the head of the long bone – the humerus in the arm or the femur in the leg – is shaped like a ball, and fits into a socket in the shape of a cup. The hip and shoulder joints are very similar as the bones that connect are covered with cartilage, and reinforced and held together with ligaments. However, the shoulder joint has more freedom than the hip and is capable of a bigger and more varied range of movement.

The shoulder joint, and to a lesser extent the hip, can perform flexion, extension, adduction, abduction and rotation. All of these movements can be performed quite easily in the shoulder as the head of the humerus can be rotated either forwards (as when bowling in cricket) or backwards (such as when swimming back crawl).

The shoulder can also be extended, as when a swimmer swings the arm backwards from the shoulder joint in preparation for a racing dive, and flexed when they bring it forward as they dive into the water. The shoulder can also adduct and abduct the upper limb. The hip is another example of a ball and socket joint but you only need to know about the shoulder for the exam.

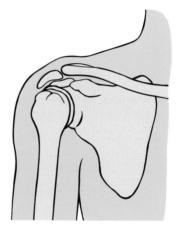

Movement possibilities at joints
Most of the movement possibilities you need to know for the examination have already been named and examples given. As well as remembering them, it is important that you can apply them to different activities by being able to work out which movement has taken place.

- The hip and shoulder are both ball and socket joints, so they have the same potential movements.

- The elbow and knee are both hinge joints, so they too have the same potential movement possibilities.

To work out what movements are possible at both joints you must firstly think of the possibilities.

156

How to work them out

If the angle of the joint is getting smaller then the movement is **flexion**.

If the angle at the joint is getting bigger then the movement is **extension**.

If the movement is taking away from the body then the movement is **abduction**.

If the action is adding to the body then the movement is **adduction**.

If the movement is around then the movement is **rotation**.

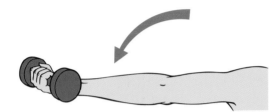

Extension

Flexion

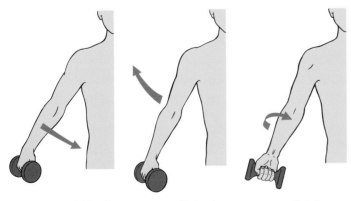

Adduction   *Abduction*   *Rotation*

ResultsPlus
Build Better Answers

(a)   Name the type of synovial joint at A, B and C.
(i)   A (shoulder) (1)
(ii) B (elbow) (1)
(iii) C (knee) (1)

Answer: (i)   A – Ball and socket

(ii) B – Hinge/Pivot

(iii) C – Hinge

Examiner's comment: You need to know these three joints and be able to identify them. Also, the answer to elbow and knee is the same.

Plantar and dorsi flexion occur around the ankle joint. Plantar flexion increases the angle, as happens when pointing the toes. Dorsi flexion decreases the angle, as happens for example when raising and lowering the heels on the edge of a step.

34: Exercise and the skeletal system

Objectives

In this chapter you will learn about the impact of physical activity and exercise on the skeletal system, including:

- the effects of long-term and regular participation in exercise and physical activity
- the importance of weight-bearing exercise in preventing osteoporosis.

The effects of exercise and physical activity on bones

Bones continue to grow and strengthen until about the age of 18, when most people have attained their adult height. Regular exercise helps bones to develop and become strong.

- Exercise can increase bone density. When bones become heavier they also become stronger.
- Ligaments (which attach bone to bone) and tendons (which attach bone to muscle) become thicker and stronger. This increases joint flexibility and allows more power in movement.

However, young people should not do too much of some types of exercise, such as weight training and long-distance running, as it can cause the bones of people who are still growing to develop unevenly.

The importance of weight-bearing exercise

Bones become lighter with age and their density and strength are gradually reduced. Although this occurs naturally, it can be a problem if too much bone is lost, resulting in a weak skeleton and bones which can break easily. This condition is called **osteoporosis**. Exercise which strengthens the bones can prevent osteoporosis, or delay its onset. Weight-bearing exercises, such as walking, running, tennis, and aerobics are good as they put weight and

pressure on certain bones, increasing their strength. Exercises that are not weight-bearing are swimming, where the body is supported by water and cycling, where the body is supported by a bike.

Yoga is another useful weight-bearing exercise as it can also improve balance, reducing the chances of falling.

Apply it!

The National Osteoporosis Society says: 'The good news is you can usually avoid osteoporosis'.

Using the points mentioned above, design a poster to encourage people to avoid osteoporosis.

Facts about bones:

- they are alive: a child's skeleton is replaced cell by cell every two years
- they stop growing in length after about age 16–18 but continue to increase in density (weight)
- they deteriorate from about the age of 35.

In summary
Weight bearing exercises are best for bones.

They include:
skipping   jumping
running up and down stairs   brisk walking.
ball games

Weight training is good for building stronger bones, but too much weight training while still growing can have a negative effect.

35: Injuries to the skeletal system and the importance of diet

Objectives

By the end of this chapter you should understand:

- the potential for injuries such as fractures and joint injuries
- common treatments for injuries (RICE)
- the importance of diet, including the effect of calcium on bones.

Injuries to bones

It is in the nature of sport that people will sometimes hurt themselves, even when every possible precaution has been taken.

Fractures

A fracture is a broken or cracked bone. Fractures can occur from a blow, e.g. to the tibia, or from a severe twisting or wrenching of a joint, e.g. at the fibula. The tibia and fibula are the long bones between knee and ankle.

The symptoms are likely to include pain at the site of the injury and, if the injured part is a limb, an inability to move it. The point of injury will be very tender and swelling might occur with bruising later. Another obvious symptom might be deformity (a misshapen bone at the point of the break); the clavicle (collar bone) is a good example Sometimes, the bone can be heard breaking.

There are several types of fracture. In **closed** fractures, as the name implies, the skin over the break is not damaged. In **compound** fractures, the broken bone protrudes through the skin. These fractures are generally more serious, as there is a risk of infection.

Simple fractures take place in one line, with no displacement of the bone. They include greenstick fractures, where the bone is only partly broken. These are common at the wrist joint, and can occur for example when running relays and using the walls to turn in the sports hall. Greenstick fractures are particularly common in children, whose bones are soft and less likely to break completely.

Stress fractures are often referred to as overuse injuries. They can happen as a result of muscles becoming fatigued and unable to absorb shock. Stress fractures can also occur when increasing the amount or intensity of exercise too rapidly or by playing on unfamiliar surfaces, e.g. switching from a soft grass tennis court to a hard court. Stress fractures can be caused by wearing ill-fitting or poor quality shoes, for example, running on hard roads and not wearing good quality running shoes. Most stress fractures happen in weight bearing parts of the body, such as the bones of the lower leg.

It has been shown that people who take part in repetitive activities which are often performed on hard surfaces, such as tennis, basketball, and road running, are susceptible to stress fractures. Rest between exercise sessions is essential to allow bones and especially joints to recover before the next training session.

Stress fractures are also linked with osteoporosis in old age and the eating disorders anorexia and bulimia.

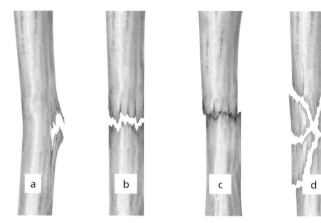

a. *greenstick – break only part way across the bone*

b. *transverse – break straight across*

c. *impacted – pieces locked into each other*

d. *comminuted – broken into more than two pieces*

e. *oblique – break at an angle*

Note: students will only be examined on the fractures mentioned on p. 158

Injuries to joints

Joints are where two or more bones meet. They are particularly prone to injury because movement past the range allowed can tear or pull tendons and ligaments. Frequent repetitive exercise can also often result in injury to joints.

Tennis and golfer's elbow

Both these conditions are overuse injuries to the tendons at the elbow joints. The main symptom of tennis elbow is pain on the outside of the elbow; it is often caused by using a racquet with the wrong sized grip. Golfer's elbow involves pain on the inside of the elbow.

Dislocations

A dislocation is when a bone at a joint is forced out of its normal position, often as a result of a hard blow which causes one of the bones to be displaced. The most obvious sign is deformity and swelling of the joint, which is locked in position. Dislocations are very painful. There may also be an associated fracture of one of the bones; if there is any doubt, the injury should be treated as a fracture.

Sprains

A sprain is a damaged ligament. One of the most common sprains in sport is a twisted ankle, which is often sustained in invasion games such as hockey, football, and rugby. A sprained ankle means that the foot has been inverted or turned inwards, tearing the ligaments which hold the bones of the ankle joint together.

Sprains often occur when stretching too far past the normal range of a joint, but can also be caused by falling, twisting or colliding with another player. Sprains of the ankle and knee are the most common, but sprains can also occur at the wrist or elbow as a result of falling and landing awkwardly.

ResultsPlus
Exam Question Report

What type of injury is a twisted ankle?
(1 mark, June 2008)

A Fracture
B Deep bruising
C Strain
D Sprain

Answer: D. Sprain.

How students answered

Some students answered this incorrectly, but actually only quite a small number of candidates (15%). Students should remember that you sprain a joint e.g. the ankle joint and you strain a muscle. Some students got this mixed up for this question.

15%   0 marks

Most students answered this well, with 85% getting this correct. This means that you need to get these types of questions correct, especially when they come up as the early multiple choice questions

85%   1 mark

Torn cartilage

Cartilage is a firm elastic substance found at the ends of the bones of a synovial joint. Tearing it, for example at the knee, can often be caused by pivoting on one foot. If a cartilage has been torn, the sufferer will usually fall to the ground. The inside of the knee will be painful, and the knee joint is likely to be bent.

Treatment for injuries

The RICE (Rest, Ice, Compression, Elevation) process is followed to treat minor injuries. If minor injuries are treated this way as soon as they occur, they can often be prevented from getting worse. Obviously, if a major injury such as a fracture or dislocation is suspected, medical help should be called.

The RICE process

1. **Rest** – stop playing or training.

2. **Ice** – using a bag of peas from the freezer, cold water or ice cubes, apply pressure to the injury. Be careful not to do this for too long as it can damage the skin. The cold can provide some pain relief and limits swelling (which can slow down the healing process) by reducing blood flow to the injured area.

3. **Compression** – use pressure to hold the ice pack on the injury. This also limits swelling and may sometimes provide pain relief.

4. **Elevation** – raise the injury, and keep it raised. Again, this helps to reduce swelling.

One way to help prevent certain injuries is by making sure bones stay strong and healthy by eating a balanced diet.

> **edexcel ::: key terms**
>
> **RICE:** Rest, ice, compression, elevation (a method of treating injuries)

ResultsPlus
Exam Question Report

Which of the following sports injuries would be treated using RICE? (1 mark, June 2008))

A Fracture
B Concussion
C Sprain
D Hypothermia

Answer C. Sprain

How students answered

Very few students got this wrong (only 3%) so it is another question that you must get correct in the examination. Even if you didn't know the answer straight away as a multiple choice question you should really be able to work the answer out to this one.

| | 3% | 0 marks |

Most students did well at this question. This means that candidates who got a G grade and above probably got this correct. If you want an A*-C you must get these questions correct

| | 97% | 1 mark |

Diet and the skeletal system

Diet is essential for a strong, healthy skeletal system.

- Eating a balanced calcium-rich diet helps the bones to grow and increase in density. The best sources of calcium are milk, cheese, and yoghurt – but choose the low fat varieties.

- Vitamin D is essential to the growth and maintenance of healthy bones and helps with the absorption of calcium. It is made by the body when the skin is exposed to sunlight.

- Smoking and too much alcohol have a toxic effect on bones.

LINK IT UP!

Refer to CH 17 to see how else your diet can improve your health.

Apply it!

Which foodstuffs provide us with the mineral we require to keep our bones healthy, particularly when we are young and when we are getting old?

Which condition are old people likely to suffer from if they lack this mineral in their diet?

ResultsPlus
Exam Question Report

The correct type of exercise can help to strengthen bones. Suggest another way in which John can maintain the strength of his bones throughout his life. (1 mark, June 2006)

Answer The correct answer is: to have calcium in his diet

How students answered

The majority of those not gaining a mark was due to the failure to mention 'calcium', referring instead to nutrients in general terms, or mentioning specific food items such as milk. The lack of further explanation meant that credit could not be given.

▓▓▓▓▓	38% 0 marks

Two out of every three students got this right so it is very important to know this as it is one of the easier questions

▓▓▓▓▓▓▓▓	62% 1 mark

examzone

Know Zone
Topic 1.2.5: A healthy, active lifestyle and your skeletal system

In this topic you will learn how your lifestyle affects your skeletal system, what happens when you take regular exercise, and the effects of exercising over a long period of time, for example when performing a PEP on a regular basis. You will also learn about types of injuries, how to recognise certain injuries that can affect the skeletal system, and how your diet can help to keep your bones in good health.

You should know...

- ☐ The functions of the skeleton and how they relate to physical activity.
- ☐ The ranges of movement possible at a hinge and ball and socket joint (flexion, extension, abduction, adduction and rotation).
- ☐ The effects of long-term and regular participation in exercise and physical activity on the skeletal system.
- ☐ The importance of weight-bearing exercise in preventing osteoporosis,
- ☐ The potential for injuries such as fractures and their treatment.
- ☐ The importance of diet, including the effect of calcium on the skeletal system.

Examiner's tip

It is to be hoped that you have not suffered any of the injuries mentioned in this topic, but you could note when other people, often top sportsmen and women, are injured. Your personal exercise programme should give you some positive benefits from taking part, especially in weight-bearing exercise and weight training. Make sure you can recall these benefits for the examination and be able to apply your knowledge if required to do so in the questions.

Key terms

RICE

Tennis elbow	Extesion
Golfer's elbow	Flexion
Fracture	Abduction
Sprain	Adduction
Strain	Rotation
Dislocation	Osteoporosis

Stretch activity

You could note in your PEP what in your diet provides your calcium (a mineral) requirement to help build more bone strength. You could also include some information about people who suffer injuries associated with the skeletal system: footballers fracture bones, rugby players dislocate shoulders. Remember the link with the principles of training, rest, and recovery and that if you get injured the principle of reversibility takes place.

Support activity

Much of this topic is about learning the types of injury that can happen to the skeletal system, how to recognise them, and the sports activities with which they are associated, e.g. golfer's elbow. Remember the long-term effects (benefits) of weight-bearing exercise in terms of 'bone health'. You could draw a table, listing all the injuries down the side and explaining how they might occur.

Question:

(a) What type of sports injuries or conditions have the following common symptoms?
(i) Swelling of tissue, distortion of natural shape and difficulty in moving the injured part. (1)
(ii) Pain around the elbow. (1)

(b) (i) What types of injuries are treated using RICE? (1)
(ii) What do the letters R.I.C.E. stand for? (1)

Students' answer	Examiners' comments	Build Better Answers
Soft tissue injuries and tennis or golfer's elbow	Incorrect. 57% of the candidates got this wrong. It is a one word answer but you must know it.	Fracture was the correct answer although dislocation is acceptable.
Broken arm	This is wrong. A lot of candidates scored 0 for this question. This is another simple application question. Tennis and golfer's elbow are very common joint injuries that students should know about and be able to apply.	Tennis or golfer's elbow was the correct answer but tendonitis is also acceptable.
Sprained ankle	This is wrong. Two thirds of the candidates got this wrong. RICE is a very common term and students must know it, when to apply it and what the letters stand for.	The answer required was 'soft tissue' as the question asked for the TYPE of injury.
Rest Ice Compression Elevation	This is the correct answer. Nearly a third of the students did not know what the letters R.I.C.E. stand for.	

The percentage of dropped marks on these multiple choice and short answers questions means dropped marks on some of the easy questions. Students must know the terminology, and be able to recall these terms in the examination. Questions on these topics almost always come up in a similar format. Four marks were available in these questions and students should be able to score well on them.

Practice Exam Questions

1 What body tissue adds stability to the knee joint? (1)

2 John is training for rugby and he dislocates his shoulder. Explain what a dislocation is. (1)

3 Sports performers may suffer a range of sports injuries.
Select one of the letters A, B, C or D for the correct combinations of injuries. (1)

A Sprain, strain, concussion   B Tennis elbow, strain, concussion

C Tennis elbow, sprain, strain   D Tennis elbow, golfer's elbow, sprain, strain, concussion

4 Which injuries would normally be associated with badminton? (1)

5 Which of these nutrients aids bone development? (1)
Fibre   Minerals   Carbohydrate

The longer answer question

Remember, in your GCSE Physical Education theory paper, the questions are always set out in the same order:

- Question 1 is split into ten multiple choice questions on all parts of the specification.
- Next comes a series of short answer questions
- Finally the longer answer question comes at the end of the paper

Tackling the longer answer questions

Don't panic when you first look at the question. There is more to write, but there are specific things the question is asking you to do. Once you find these, answering the question becomes easier.

Try to think through these questions in the following order:

1. Check your time
2. Read the question
3. Recall your knowledge
4. Apply your knowledge
5. Write your answer
6. Check your answer

And remember – don't waffle!

These stages were explained in more detail on p. 92-3.

Example question

Louise is a sprinter and long jumper and she is taking GCSE Physical Education and has to plan, perform, monitor and evaluate her own Personal Exercise Programme (PEP) during her PE course. Although she plans to do some specialist training to improve her sprinting and long jumping, she also plans to include some circuit training in order to maintain and improve her all round fitness. Two of the exercises she has included are press ups and step ups onto a bench.

Identify and describe which specific aspect of Heath Related-Exercise this will improve. Then identify, describe and explain – making sure that you use the correct terminology – which muscles are working and how they work together during each exercise.

Answering the question

1. **Check the time**

2. **Read the question**

   Look at exactly what the question is asking you to do and break it down into smaller parts.

   Part 1 is asking you to identify which component of health-related exercise will improve. It's about the muscles and maintaining their fitness and improving it. Circuit training is not going to improve the ability of the muscle to lift heavy weights (muscular strength) but it will improve the ability of the muscles to work harder for longer and that is the **description** of muscular endurance. Therefore put this in your answer with a description.

3. **Recall your knowledge**

   Part 2 in this question is the recall part and in this case it is about the muscles. You must know them well as they are either correct or wrong. **Identify** – the muscles working in the press-ups are the biceps and the triceps. The quadriceps and hamstrings are the muscles working in the step-ups. **You must then describe** where they are there is no obvious choice it is either correct or wrong

4. **Apply your knowledge**

   Well the word to focus on here is **explain** (how they work together) using the correct terminology. The terminology is the names of the muscles and the word used to describe how they work – antagonistic.

5. **Write your answer**

   You have the areas you need to write about, now structure your answer logically through the order of the question, i.e. answer the health related exercise part first then explain the press up and then explain the step up

6. **Finally read and check your answer to make sure your have included everything and that it is well written.**

   You must include everything that is asked in the question but don't waffle. These questions may have a lot of space available to write your answer but don't think you have to keep on writing because there is still some space available. Structure your answer and give what is required.

Model student answer

In her Personal Exercise Programme (PEP) Louise will be improving her muscular endurance which will enable the voluntary muscles she is exercising to be able to work harder for longer without getting tired.

Press up: In the press ups she will use her biceps in the front of the upper arm and the triceps at the back of the upper arm to work antagonistically (in pairs) with the biceps flexing the arm to control the downward movement and the triceps extending her arm and pushing her body upwards.

Step ups: In the step ups the muscles working are the quadriceps, at the front of the upper leg, which will extend straightening the legs as they step up onto the bench and the hamstring flexing at the back of the leg controlling the downward movement and these muscles will work as antagonistic pairs.

ResultsPlus
Watch out!

Don't use shortened versions of the names of the muscles, use quadriceps not quads, use pectorals not pecs, latissimus dorsi not lats etc.

As pointed out above don't waffle, structure your answer and stick to the point. This answer can be fitted into half a page of the question paper.

This question wants you to use the term antagonistic, and to explain it. Not using the correct terms here will mean you lose marks.

Mark scheme

The points below are the answers the examiner will be looking for:

   identifying health-related exercise component and description

   correctly identifying biceps and triceps and correctly describing where they are

   correctly identifying quadriceps and hamstrings correctly describing where they are

   getting the correct muscles with the correct exercise

   explaining how antagonistic pairs (terminology) of muscles work

   a well constructed answer

Unit 2: Performance in Physical Education

Unit 2 Performance in Physical Education is the practical elements of the course and this will provide 60% of your final grade. It is sub-divided into smaller parts as follows:

- The **practical performance** makes up 48% of your final grade. You must show your ability in four sports, up to three roles. These roles are: practical performer, leader and official.

- The **analysis of performance** must be on one of your chosen practical activities and must be an analysis of a practical performer (not of an official or a leader).

- The final area of the Analysis of Performance is the personal exercise programme, which you must plan, perform, monitor and evaluate. This is a requirement for every student.

Short course
If you are taking the short course you can offer one performance and one as an official or a leader but that must come from a different activity group e.g. performance in athletics and officiate in football.

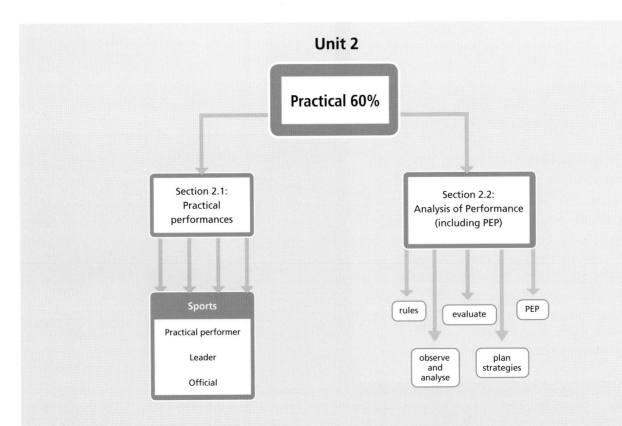

Section 2.1: Practical performance

The practical performance part of the course makes up 48 per cent of the total marks in both the short and full courses, so you need to do well at this to get a top grade. You will need to know:

- what you will do in this part of the course

- how you will be assessed

- which activities you can offer.

> **edexcel ⫶ examiner tip**
> Breaking the course down will enable you to assess your standard in each part and your potential exam grade. You should set goals for each section so that you can achieve your best possible grade in the exam.

What will I do in this part of the course?

There are two courses you could be taking: the Full Course GCSE (referred to as 2PE01) or the Short Course (3PE01).

In the full course you will be examined on four practical activities; in the short course you will be examined on two.

Your school may teach you more than four practical activities (or more than two in the short course). This could be because at first neither you nor your teacher are sure exactly which activities are most likely to get you the highest marks in the exam. By the time you have completed four or five practical activities you should have a good idea of your standard in each.

How will I be assessed

You will be entered for the practical controlled assessment task and moderation, which usually take place between March and May in the year of your exam. Your final mark for each practical activity will come from this practical assessment on moderation day, which will be organised by your school and attended by a visiting moderator. The moderator may be present for all four of your practical activities or just for some of them, depending usually on number of people from your school taking the course. However, your teachers will mark you in each activity.

During the assessment you will be set tasks by your teachers. These will range from individual skills to game-type practices, games, and the final performance. These tasks will vary according to the activity, but wherever possible will allow you to show the best of your ability.

168

So what activities can I offer?

The activities you can choose are clearly set out in the Controlled Assessment Guide. They fall into six different groups. You must choose from at least two different groups, but you do not have to include an activity from every group; for example, you could choose three activities from one group and one from another.

Your school will probably be able to offer a selection of these activities. It may also allow you to include one or more out-of-school sports, such as horse riding, karate, or swimming, in your chosen activities. You should talk to your teacher about this, as special arrangements will be necessary both during the course and when assessing your final mark.

You can offer your activities in three ways:

● as a practical performer

● as a leader

● as an official.

You must be a practical performer in at least two of your activities. In the other two, you could be an official, or a leader, or an official in one and a leader in the other. You could even be a practical performer, a leader, and an official in one activity, but your fourth choice must then be as a practical performer in an activity from a different group.

If you are offering officiating or leading then you will be asked to officiate or lead in the chosen activity on moderation day. You will also need to provide evidence of the level at which you have experienced these roles during the course. This might be, for example, a log book recording your involvement in coaching at a club, or matches you have refereed. The marking criteria will be similar to those used in marking practical performance.

How will I be marked?

Each practical activity is marked out of 10 against criteria set out in a book called the Controlled Assessment Guide, which you can look at on the Edexcel website. Each practical activity mark is worth 12 per cent of the 60 per cent of your overall practical mark; this means that your practical activities are worth 48 per cent of your total mark.

While you are performing on moderation day, your teacher will mark you on each aspect of the tasks, using the criteria in the Controlled Assessment Guide. The moderator will do the same.

> **edexcel ⬛ examiner tip**
> It is a good idea to be familiar with the Controlled Assessment Guide for your chosen activities. Knowing what you need to do to get a 10 can make all the difference.

TARGET SETTING FOR PRACTICAL ACTIVITIES

Target setting is important because it will help you understand how to get the best possible results. In the long course you will get four practical marks, in the short course you will get two. Re-read the previous pages to refresh your memory on how the practical activities are assessed.

Understanding the marking criteria
These are set out in bands:

1–2; 3–4; 5–6; 7–8; and 9–10.

Performance marking criteria are different for each activity. Marking criteria for officiating and leading are the same for every activity.

You will usually be marked against each band for your competence in each particular skill. These marks are averaged to give your overall band mark.

For example, Lela is performing basketball. She has been marked in the 7–8 band for passing, but in the 5–6 band for dribbling and shooting, and a 6 in the game situation. On this basis Lela would probably be marked as a high 6. She would not merit a 7 because most of her performance was in the 5–6 band, with 7–8 only for passing, and a 6 in the game situation.

Look up the bands for your own chosen activities by going to the practical criteria for each.

How to get a better mark

Choose one of your practical activities, and look up the marking criteria for it on the Edexcel website. Give yourself an honest mark against how you are currently performing at your chosen sport. Ask others for feedback. Ask your teacher what he or she thinks. Once you have established a realistic band, ask yourself why you are not at the next level. In the basketball example above, Lela might ask herself why she is not a 7–8 and ask herself and her teacher why she only got 6 for the game situation. The reason might be that her passing is good enough but her dribbling and shooting are not. When you understand why you are not at a higher level, you can work on improving your weak points. Lela might aim to work at her dribbling and shooting skills and that should help her contribution to the game.

This process will help you understand your strengths and weaknesses. It could help you identify how to improve and then measure your improvement. This will motivate you and give you a sense of achievement, which is essential to success in performance. By doing this, you are learning to analyse performance.

Task

Study the Controlled Activity Guide for your first activity and work out what mark you could expect if you took the exam now.

Now think about the points you need to work on in order to improve to the next grade or band, and list the ways in which you could do this.

Example: basketball

1. I think that I am in the 5–6 band now.
2. In order to reach the 7–8 band I must improve in the following ways:

   dribbling – become effective with either hand

   passing – improve my ability to use variety and deception and learn to signal effectively and with good timing

   lay-up – improve my left hand dribbling and drive from the weaker side, but I may lay-up with my weaker hand

   jump shot – learn to point to the ring in my follow through and land in the correct position

   game – improve my ability to exploit openings and threaten opponents by scoring and/or assisting.
3. In order to do this I will:
   - work hard
   - pay special attention to these aspects in the lessons
   - attend basketball practices.

This task should be completed before the start of each practical activity.

Section 2.2: Analysis of Performance

Overview: What is the analysis of performance (AoP)?

You may have had some practice at analysing performance during Key Stage 3, but it was probably called evaluation. At GCSE level, analysis of performance (AoP) is designed to help you apply the knowledge you have gained throughout the course by watching and analysing another player's performance. Many students become quite expert at this part of the course and score high marks, while others may find it very difficult. The good news is that you can practise and improve your ability at the AoP in many ways.

What will I have to do?

The AoP is carried out in one of the activities you are offering in the role of player/performer; it cannot be based upon the role of official or leader. You will need to watch another player's performance and give feedback in the following areas.

1. Rules, regulations, and terminology

The first section of the AoP criteria is on 'Rules, regulations, and terminology'. You will need to know these, and for the higher marks you will also need to show a clear understanding of them and to apply them.

2. Observe and analyse performance

In the second section you will observe the performance and give a detailed analysis using suitable techniques for the activity and the correct technical terminology. You will then use what you have learned from your analysis in your feedback, whether written or oral.

3. Evaluate performance

In the third section you will be required to evaluate in detail what you have observed and analysed. This means understanding and describing the strengths and limitations of the performance and knowing what it should look like – the 'perfect model'.

4. Plan strategies, tactics, and practices

The next section requires you to plan strategies, tactics, and practices. This means being able to feedback to the player on techniques they could use to improve their performance, so as to come closer to the perfect model. This of course will depend on what you are observing. For example if it is a game, such as netball, then tactics would probably be relevant, but if it is a skill such as a short service in badminton, practising would be important.

5. Plan a personal exercise programme

The personal exercise programme (PEP) is a training plan that will improve performance. It must be well-designed (planned), performed (by you), and monitored (recorded) over a six-week period. It must also show improvement in fitness levels. It must then be evaluated, with comments on how it benefited you and suggestions on how to develop it further.

Martin O'Neil observing a game from the touchline

How will I be assessed?

The AoP is worth 12 per cent of the total mark for your GCSE in Physical Education. This 12 per cent is divided between the five components listed above, each of which is marked out of 4 (giving a highest possible total mark of 20). The assessment is now known as a 'controlled assessment' which means you will be supervised, in curriculum time, while you do the work.

The AoP is carried out in one of the activities you have chosen to offer in the role of player/performer. Although you are likely to choose your best practical activity for your AoP, some candidates find that it is easier to analyse an activity which is not their best, as some activities are easier to analyse than others. It is a good idea to practise AoP in all of your activities.

You can choose to do your AoP in one of three ways.

1. An oral interview with your teacher carried out while you are observing a performance in the chosen AoP activity.

2. A written piece of work that you have researched. This would be written up in a timed period with your teacher, and probably other candidates from your centre, present.

3. A presentation. This would be prepared in a similar way to the written work and then presented to your teacher (other candidates may or may not be present).

Target setting for the AoP

As with the practical performance activities, it is a good idea to set targets for improving your abilities in the AoP.

The first step is to understand roughly how good you are now in each section of the AoP by giving yourself a mark out of 4. You might want to do this with your teacher, but make sure you have first read and understood the criteria for obtaining a good mark. Use **SMART** goal setting to set yourself a realistic target for each of the five sections and note what you need to do to achieve this mark. For example, it may be that you know the rules of basketball but

need some practice at applying them. In this case you might set a target to go to the Year 7 basketball club and referee during the practices.

Apply it!

Set your targets for the AoP as you would for the practical activity. Estimate your mark now in each of the five sections of the criteria and discuss it with your teacher. If you have not started your personal exercise programme yet, you will have to estimate that mark. Then work out what you need to do to reach the next level (e.g. get another two marks) and analyse how you could do it.

Use a version of the template below:

I think my AoP grade at the moment is:	
Rules	
Observing and analysing	
Evaluating	
Planning strategies, tactics and practices	
The PEP	
Estimated mark now	/20=C

I think my grade now is at level /20 = grade

I want to improve to level /20 = grade

In order to do reach my targets I need to improve in the following areas:

Then, using the SMART principle for goal setting (specific, measurable, achievable, realistic, time-based), you can set goals.

Topic 2.2.1: Rules, regulations and terminology

Sport in context

It's the final of the women's 200 metre freestyle swimming at the Olympic Games. The starter calls the competitors to their starting blocks, shouts 'take your marks', but someone dives in before the hooter sounds. What happens next? It's the Olympics Games and the rules are that the swimmer is disqualified. Why?

The rules and regulations are there to make it fair for everyone in the competition and also for the safety of the competitors. This may not be so obvious in swimming, but in combat and contact sports, for example, it is very important. In our swimming example, 'freestyle' is terminology for the swimming stroke.

What you need to do

Students need to be able to:

- demonstrate understanding of the rules
- be able to apply the rules as a player or official
- use the correct terminology and technical terms.

Rules and regulations help keep sport fair and safe. Terminology is applied to individual sports to describe many of these rules and regulations appropriately. To analyse a performance you must first know the rules and terminology, and to get the higher marks you need to show a clear understanding of them and be able to apply them.

If you have offered the activity you are analysing as an official as well as a practical performer, you should score well in this section. But remember that using the correct terminology is important in all sports, especially when you are analysing them.

Finding out about the rules and terminology

Rules are important, but different, in every sport. For example:

- in racket games there are specific rules to do with serving, receiving service, court markings, and what happens when the scores are equal

- in athletics there are commands to start sprint races and slightly different rules to start longer distance races. In the field events there are different rules for vertical and horizontal jumps. Throwing events have rules about the weight of the implements to be thrown.

Find out about the rules of your activity by looking at the website of its governing body. For example, you could find out about the rules of football by visiting the Football Association's website, www.thefa.com.

You must demonstrate that you understand the rules, can apply them, and understand the correct technical terminology; you will not gain marks if you simply download them and paste them in to your work.

Understanding and applying the terminology is very important. The criteria state that, to gain full marks on this section, students must 'show a clear understanding of the technical terms appropriate for the activity'. If you fail to use the correct terminology you will lose marks and at best be awarded 3 out of 4.

What you should know about the rules
It is best to have a clear knowledge and understanding of the rules of all your practical activities, although you will only take the AoP in one of them. A clear understanding means knowing how to recognise and interpret the rules. You must know the signals and what the penalty for the offence is; for example, in football a hand ball can mean a direct free kick or a penalty according to where the offence took place.

If your chosen activity is basketball, for example, you should be able to explain:

- what 'travelling' is (so you must know and be able to use the terminology) and when it might happen

- what the referee would do on seeing it (blow his/ her whistle)

- what the decision would be (give the ball to the other team), and the signal to indicate this decision (the referee would rotate his/her fists)

- what the other team would do with the ball (put it into play from the sideline), and where they would take the ball from (opposite to/level with where the travelling took place).

In an activity such as trampoline you would be expected to know the regulations, how many bounces there are in a routine, and how to set out a routine and calculate the tariff. In this activity there is a lot of terminology, for example in naming the different moves. One example is 'barani' that describes a front somersault with a half-twist.

Showing your understanding
When working on your own analysis of performance you could choose a contentious rule, like the off-side rule (law 11) in football, and explain it in your own way. It might help to use diagrams, digital photographs, and video as you could show your understanding of them. Using the correct terminology to explain the off-side rule, such as active and passive positions, would also gain more marks.

Task

For one of your practical activities choose one of the more difficult or controversial rules. Research the governing body website and make sure you understand the rule, then explain it, if possible using diagrams to help. For example, you could explain the off side rule in football, or write 'tariff' and explain a 10 bounce routine in trampoline.

Topic 2.2.2: Observe and analyse performance

Sport in context

Coaches are there to improve performance, but they can't do this unless they can see exactly what's going on in a game or competition. Experienced coaches such as Arsene Wenger or Sir Alex Ferguson know where they want to observe the game from and also what they are looking for and what can go wrong. Football matches are won or lost by tactics, and football coaches usually watch from the 'technical area' (the side of the pitch near the halfway line) where they can see and communicate with the players.

Skills and techniques are very important in sports such as swimming and athletics, so coaches may choose more than one viewing point – in swimming several viewing points may be best.

What you need to do

- Make a detailed observation from the best positions.

- Make a detailed analysis, recording quantitative or/and qualitative data.

- Use the data recorded to create concise, detailed feedback.

In this second section you must observe the performance and make a detailed analysis of it, using suitable techniques for the activity. Using the correct technical terminology and what you have learned from your analysis, you can then offer written or verbal feedback which could improve the participant's performance.

Observe

Referees, umpires, judges, and officials must make sure they are in the best position to judge the competition or referee the activity. A bad position can result in a wrong analysis. Observation skills can be developed in a number of ways, from watching professionals to experimenting with different angles, but most importantly you need to know what you are looking for.

Before you start your observation, you should know what the skill or activity looks like when performed perfectly – the 'perfect model'. This will help you to measure the quality of the performance you are observing. You also need to have a good idea of what can go wrong with the performance even before you observe it. As a result you know what you are looking for and what to expect.

When you are asked to analyse a performance you are being asked to observe 'how well the task is completed': remember that this is the definition of the word performance. Observing performance often requires viewing from various angles, so you do not miss a key problem or quality. In golf, for example, you may want to watch the player from the front to observe grip and stance and from behind to observe swing.

Task

Choose the skill you perform best from any sport you know. Describe in writing or by talking to a partner exactly how to perform that skill to perfection.

Analyse

To analyse means to consider something in detail. As with observation, a good understanding of the sport is essential. When analysing a performance, it is important to break it down into smaller parts, consider each part individually, then think of ways to improve it. Each part can then be practised and as each part improves, so does the performance as a whole. Finally, put the player back into the game and assess whether improvement has taken place.

Invasion games can be broken down into attack and defence, so that each part can be analysed. For example, you could start by looking at the opposing team's defensive formation. You could then look at your own team's attacking formation to analyse whether the best form of attack is being used to break down the opposing team's defence. Or if you are losing by one goal and running out of time in an important match, you might change from a 4:4:2 formation to a 4:3:3. The final score of the game, or the number of shots on target, or other written information will show whether or not the change of tactics was successful.

In racket games, forced and unforced errors could be analysed. Forced errors occur when an opponent makes a shot that you cannot get back, while an unforced error means that you have made a poor shot, such as a service fault.

Breaking down skills

All sports have skills which make up individual actions or moves such as kicking, catching, and hitting. When analysing a skill it is very important to break it down into smaller parts, analyse each part, think of ways to improve it, and build it back up again. In most sports there is a recognised way to do this. In swimming, for example, skills can be broken down into:

- body position
- leg action
- arm action
- breathing
- timing.

When analysing somebody else you should look for the good points first. Many students begin by commenting on the bad points, but most performances do have some good points, although it might be difficult to find them. Starting with the good points helps the performer's confidence. Next, look for areas for improvement. Even the best performances have areas which could be improved. There may be a number of these and you should note as many as you can. Then you need to decide which area is the most important for the performer to work on.

Apply it!

For one of your activities, choose a skill e.g. shooting in netball or a lay-up shot in basketball, and show how you would break it down into smaller parts.
1. Work out what can go wrong in each part.
2. Observe your partner performing the skill.
3. Analyse how well the task was completed (performance).

Apply it!

Observe your partner's performance and work out the areas for improvement. Then list them in order of importance, putting the one needing most improvement at the top of the list.

Recording the results of an analysis
Performance can be analysed through observation subjectively and objectively.

A **subjective** analysis means your opinion, based upon what you have seen, observed (watched carefully), and perhaps noted. Other people may have a different opinion, so you need to have subjective evidence to put your points across. This is called a **qualitative** analysis.

An **objective** analysis is based not on opinion but on fact. You have the results and statistics to prove what you have analysed. This evidence will back up your opinion from the observation and is called **quantitative** or **notational** analysis.

Both types of analysis are useful and used regularly in sport. Objective analysis is used more than subjective analysis by coaches or scouts to analyse an opposition's tactics so they know what to expect. Tactics play a big part in a team or individual's performance. There may be no or very few tactics at the lower levels of sport, but at the higher levels a great deal of time and effort is spent devising team or individual tactics, which might be changed to deal with particular opponents. In professional sport, scouts attend the games of future opponents to analyse their performance and gather information before devising tactics and deciding which players to select.

Notational analysis before a game
The practice of coaches analysing teams or individuals before a game or event is common in many sports. The coaches write a report on what they have learned and often include a lot of statistics – quantitative analysis. In invasion games these statistics might include the number of shots by each individual player, how many were on target, how many missed the target, where the successful shots came from, where the players shot from most often, the number of successful and unsuccessful passes made by each player, and the distance over which they were made. This information is then used for future games.

Notational analysis during a game
Notational analysis during a game is similar but is used during the game itself or the interval/time out. Notational analysis can be done in various ways in team games, racket, and individual sports and is often shown on television during important tournaments: the Premier League and Wimbledon are good examples.

Summary

The quality of the analysis depends on several factors. The first of these is the quality of the observation, so some preparation and/or practice needs to be done first. In the initial stages choose something simple to analyse – something you are good at and know how to do. If it is a skill, write down its different parts and then observe (watch carefully) as your partner performs it. Insert a tick or a cross in the boxes to show whether you are happy with each part of the skill, then you can check it later. Practising like this also helps you get to know and understand the perfect model and learn to measure performance against it.

Before you begin your observation and analysis, you need to know:

- **why** you want to know
- **where** you will observe from
- **what** you want to observe – skills, game/competition, fitness
- **how** you are going to do it – qualitative – quantitative – or both
- **when** you are going to do it – practice session, a game or the exam.

When analysing a performance you must know what happened and why.

Aspect of skill	Unsuccessful	Problem	Work on
Dribble	X	Head down	Head up dribble
Pick-up	+		
1-2 count	+		
Jump	+		
Release	X	Hand position	Demonstrate
Aim	X	Sighting	Lock up to backboard
Force	+		
Landing	+		
Result	X	20%	Check %

Analysis of the skills involved in a lay-up shot

Player	Points scored	Shots missed	Total points	Total misses
4	2	X	2	1
5	2	XXXXXXX	2	7
6	0	XX	0	2
7	2.3	XXXX	5	4
8	2.2.2	XX	6	2
9	2.2.3.2.3.3.2.2	XX	9	2
10	3.2	XXX	5	3
11	2	XXXXXXX	2	7

A notational analysis of a basketball team

Topic 2.2.3: Evaluate performance

When you have done your analysis you must evaluate (assess) the quality of the performance, skill, tactics, and fitness factors based upon what you have seen and any statistics you may have noted.

The perfect model

Your evaluation of a performer will be measured against the perfect model, which is how professional athletes would perform at their highest level. This knowledge may come from being involved in the sport: playing and competing in the activity, and being coached or taught by your teacher. It may also come from reading about it, watching videos, looking at photographs or posters, and watching demonstrations by good players.

Having a good knowledge of the perfect model does not necessarily mean that you can perform perfectly yourself. Many great coaches were not great performers. Knowledge of the perfect model means you understand how a performance should look, and what the outcome of a correct performance should be. This helps you to analyse skills and performance.

Evaluating a performance

Coaches often look at quantitative analysis to evaluate a performance. This is created during a game or training session and then analysed in relation to other participants and to the perfect model.

This gymnast's shape could be an example of the perfect model for others.

Evaluating a quantitative (notational) analysis of a team game.

The example below shows a quantitative analysis of a practice and game situation in football (3 v 3 with two restricted support players) looking at keeping possession of the ball.

From this quantitative (notational) analysis we can now evaluate the performance, picking out the strengths and areas for improvement. We may be happy with some players (those with a high percentage success rate) but others (those with a low percentage success rate) can be improved.

Possession

Keeping possession requires players to be able to pass and control it. To be successful at passing, players need to get the ball to another player accurately, giving them the best chance possible to control the ball. This means passing the football with a required weight because if the ball is hit too hard, or too high, the receiver is likely to lose control of the ball and give the opposition a chance to take possession.

Good control helps players to set themselves up to play an accurate pass – if the ball is too far ahead, or too high, the pass will be difficult to control. Zhia, the least successful passer, could have had problems controlling the ball which in turn affected his ability to make an accurate pass.

It is more difficult to keep possession if the player is marked by an opponent, so getting free is also part of the equation. Therefore passing the ball at the right time (when the receiver is in a space) is important. It is necessary to devise practices that involve controlling the ball in many different ways, pass it so that it is easily controlled and in a small game so that opposition is involved. This will be discussed in the next component of the AoP.

Mickey is clearly the star player. He is in the game the most and has the highest success rate in both practice and game.

How would you plan practices to improve the performance?

Player name	Successful passes	Total	Unsuccessful passes	Total	Combined	% Success rate
	Practice					
Mickey	///// ///// /////	20	//	2	22	90.90909091
Jake	///// ///// /	11	//	2	13	84.61538462
Zhia	///// ////	9	//	2	11	81.81818182
	Game				0	
Mickey	///// ///// //	12	//	2	14	85.71428571
Jake	///	3	/	1	4	75
Zhia	///// /	6	//	2	8	75
	Practice and game					
Mickey		32		4	36	88.88888889
Jake		14		3	17	82.35294118
Zhia		15		4	19	78.94736842

Evaluation of a performance in an individual activity such as swimming

100 metres freestyle	Time for each	Accumulative time in seconds	25 metre pool
1	15.2	15.2	25m
2	15.5	30.7	50m
3	15.5	46.2	75m
4	16.1	62.3	100m

A swimming notational analysis on fitness, time, and performance might look like the table.

What will an evaluation of this analysis show?

- The first length was the fastest.
- The fourth length was the slowest.
- The second and third lengths were the same.
- The second and third lengths were slower than the first but faster than the last.

It would help to know:

1. the swimmer's personal best time
2. their final position in the race
3. their position at the end of each length.

From this analysis your evaluation might be that there is a lack of fitness as the last length was far slower than the first. This could suggest that there is a problem with tactics; the swimmer should have gone a little slower on the first length to try to achieve more equal splits. The term 'split' is the correct terminology; it is important to use the correct terminology as often as possible to show that you know and understand the activity well.

From your analysis you may also have evaluated the swimmer's technique and skills. When evaluating elements of a performance remember how to break down the skill and analyse it. Using the swimming example, this might mean that in your evaluation you have seen that the leg kick needs to improve or it might be that the 'tumble' turns were slow and added more time to each length so need to be improved. Using the expression 'tumble turn' again demonstrates that you know the correct terminology, which shows a strong understanding of the sport and will help you score higher marks.

Evaluating skills

Each skill, such as swimming front crawl, can be broken down into a number of individual parts. Each part has to be performed correctly according to the perfect model as any problems may influence other parts and prevent a good result.

In swimming we should consider the swimmer's body position first. If you watch a video of Eric 'the eel' Mousabami, who swam in the Sydney Olympic in 2000, you would see a poor body position: his hips are too low, the knees are bent, and the swimmer is not kicking from the hips. These parts are linked; the poor leg kick is causing the poor body position. To improve this position his trainer would have to develop a practice to strengthen and improve the leg kick, then the body position should also show improvement. Michael Phelps, on the other hand demonstrates great technique and strength, therefore he would be an ideal perfect model to evaluate Eric Mousabami against.

Topic 2.2.4: Plan strategies, tactics and practices

Planning means working out ways to improve a performance: how you do this will depend on what needs to be improved. Skills may be improved through practices or drills which you could have learned from a teacher or a book, or devised yourself. A difficult or new skill may have to be broken down and learned piece by piece before being put back together again. Passing in football (and other team games) is a good example of this.

The football quantitative analysis table on p. 179 records passes where players practised keeping possession, first in a training session then in a game. The quantitative analysis shows that Zhia has the least successful pass rate in relation to his number of passes. This could be a result of various problems with his skills (as mentioned above the table). Based on this quantitative analysis and an understanding of the problem, practices, tactics, and strategies could then be planned.

You may find more than one problem when analysing and evaluating a skill, so you must decide which is the most important and work on correcting this one first. You can then decide what to work on next, and so on. You may decide improving one skill is also likely to improve another. Once the skill has been improved the participant should be put under pressure, in the football example this would be with a defender or defenders in opposition, as would happen in a game.

Planning practices

Zhia will probably benefit from practising control and passing first. So you might decide on the following course of action.

1. Start by practising planned passing and control with various parts of the body such as, head, thighs, and feet in a fairly static position. Zhia could start with a simple feed, knowing that the ball will be coming along the ground to his feet. As it arrives he will offer his foot to the ball and caress, withdrawing his foot to take the power out of the pass, getting the ball under control. You may need to break the skill down and practise each part, then build it back up again into the full skill.

2. When waiting to receive the pass from a server he should be working out where/whom he is going to pass it to. In the first case it might be back to the server but later it may be that he has to turn and pass it to a third player so he will have to work out how he is going to perform that manoeuvre. In a game a player should always be thinking, 'if the ball comes to me now what options do I have? What is the best option?'

3. Introduce more difficult serving and some movement to the player, but still no opposition. Zhia will not know what type of ball he will need to control and the server will start to pass the ball at different distances/speeds.

When he has improved this part of the practice, gradually introduce passive opposition forcing him to take that into account 'how will I control the ball'. This way he will learn to shield it from the opposition and adjust his position to keep control of the ball, as well as needing to get into position to pass it to a team mate.

As a coach you may stop Zhia at certain points to explain how well he has done or how he could have performed better.

As this improves more difficult services can be introduced e.g. so Zhia will not know how the ball will arrive and will have to make the decision as to what part of his body he will use to control it and keep it from the opposition.

4. Follow this with a small sided game where the team in possession has more players so it is easier for them, perhaps 5 v 3 so there will be lots of options. After a while reduce it to 4 v 3 and eventually 3 v 3.

5. Follow this with a real game.

   Ask yourself whether the performer has improved. Record another quantitative analysis to show if he has improved or not. Motivate him. In the original practice game 1 in every 4 of Zhia's passes went to the opposition so he should try to improve on this.

You can apply your theory knowledge while creating a plan, especially the HRE and SRF. For example, what skills will Zhia need to help him control the ball: you may consider balance, coordination and reaction time as being three that he will definitely need. Can you explain how he will use them? And how a practice could be designed to improve them?

Apply it!

1. Choose a skill which is essential to one of your practical activities, then name three faults which might occur when practising it. List them in order of importance, and then devise a method of improving them similar to the example above.

2. In the activity you are practising at present, state how you will set about improving your skills performance.

Planning your own strategies, tactics or practices

What you focus on in this section will depend on what you have chosen to analyse. If it is a team game you may want to improve a number of individual skills, strategies, and tactics. If this is the case you must plan practices to develop these skills. For example, if you found that the passing was poor you might plan a new strategy to improve 'support' for the player in possession. This new strategy would give the player in possession more options when under pressure from the other team. Alternatively, you may want to develop a strategy focusing on possession and 'control', so players under pressure can keep the ball better without support.

If you are planning to improve a skill in an individual sport, you probably want to work on practices. For example, watching a swimmer doing the front crawl, you may have observed that the body position was poor and that this was caused by a poor leg kick. To remedy this, you would plan practices to improve the swimmer's leg kick action, working specifically on the technique. This could be done by practising kicking movements while holding a float; this focused practice, with no arm movements, should improve the swimmer's leg kick action, bringing it closer to the perfect model. If you think that the swimmer would benefit from a stronger leg kick and a stronger pull in the arm action (especially in the final 25 metres) then some work on fitness would also be appropriate. Circuit training would be an ideal method that would allow you to focus on working both the arms and legs. This decision could be made using similar results to those recorded on p. 180 evaluating the quantitative analysis of a swimmer.

One way to improve your chosen skill could be through developing your fitness. This would probably be done in a personal exercise programme (PEP) designed to improve fitness over six weeks.

Feedback

Getting information is one thing; passing it on so it can be used to improve performance is another. Some coaches are very good at analysing individual and team performances but not at conveying the information to their players or team so that they understand what is required of them.

Good coaches might use a combination of positive and negative feedback. Some people respond best to lots of encouragement while being quietly told how to improve their play or tactics, while some respond to being told clearly what they did wrong. Feeding back information is a skill which coaches need to work on to get the best results.

What to feedback

When coaching there may be several things to say all at the same time, and the coach must select what is most important. Feedback to a gymnast is more likely to be on skills than on tactics, but a half-time team talk in rugby is almost certain to include tactics. Feedback after a game might include comments on the player's fitness, effort or temperament.

When to feedback

In many situations feedback may be immediate: during a game for example, at half-time or a time out. Most coaches will also give some general feedback after the activity has finished. During a training session feedback is generally continuous, especially if it is a session designed to improve a specific skill. Coaches also give feedback on the last match, and again just before a competition.

How can we feedback? And how often should we feedback?

As well as feeding back verbally, visually, and through demonstrations, good coaches ask the performers for their opinions and ideas. Remember feedback must be designed to get the best out of the player and improve performance.

Topic 2.2.5: Plan a personal exercise programme (PEP)

Your personal exercise programme (PEP) shows exactly how you have improved your fitness.

You should use the theoretical knowledge you gained earlier in the course to help you create a personal exercise programme which will gradually enhance your performance in the activity you have chosen by focusing on an area of fitness you want to improve. Your personal exercise programme should include:

● components of health-related exercise (HRE)

● components of skill-related fitness (SRF)

● principles of training

● methods of training

● goal setting.

The personal exercise programme is closely related to the analysis of performance. If you are using one of your own activities in your analysis of performance, your personal exercise programme will be designed to improve that activity. If you have chosen to analyse someone else's performance, you should be able to apply the knowledge gained from your personal exercise programme.

For example, the training programme planned for the swimmer on p. 181 could be adapted so as to improve the swimmer's speed, strength, and stamina. This would allow the swimmer to perform better in future races, especially in the final length. The new programme might be planned to cover a six-week period. After this time, the swimmer's performance could be analysed again and this analysis compared with the first.

Designing your personal exercise programme

To start the plan you should use two principles of training:

● individual needs/differences

● specificity

to clarify which aspects of fitness (taken from health-related exercise and skill-related fitness) need to be improved. For example, the swimmer will probably need to work on muscular endurance in the legs and arms, to aid the kick and pull of the front crawl, and cardiovascular fitness to help stamina.

When you have decided which aspects of fitness you are going to work on, you need to look at how you intend to do this. Use what you have learned about the methods of training, FITT, and goal setting to help you.

● The FITT principle helps you determine how often you should train, how hard, and for how long, and also what type of training you should choose.

● Setting goals and applying SMART targets will help ensure that your plan can be achieved and that you stay motivated. For example, by setting SMART goals, the swimming coach might realise that the swimmer is only likely to improve slightly over six weeks, as he or she is only able to train twice a week.

You must choose suitable training methods. The swimmer will probably use continuous training to help endurance, but the programme is also likely to include interval training to improve speed. Some land conditioning in the form of weight training might be included, and almost certainly some circuit training to work on the strength and endurance of specific muscles used while swimming. If several methods are used, the swimmer is doing cross training.

You also need to outline what you will do in your sessions: your warm-up and cool-down, and your main activities in each method. If you are circuit training, you could produce a circuit training card to show what you will do at each station, with photographs of yourself doing the activity and an explanation of what is involved.

You should try to use progressive overload and allow enough rest and recovery time. Over the six-week period, the swimmer's coach would use progressive overload so that the programme gradually becomes harder (perhaps increasing in difficulty every two weeks) as the swimmer gets fitter. Some rest and recovery must be built in to the programme to allow the swimmer's body to adapt to the training and also try to avoid injury or illness so that no training sessions are missed and the swimmer does not lose fitness (reversibility).

Everything you achieve in a training session should be recorded and reviewed against your targets. In the example, the planned target could be for the swimmer's time to improve over 100 metres. On the way to achieving this target, other results would be measured: these could include the swimmer's best time over 25 and 50 metres, working heart rate as a guide to how hard the swimmer is working, and

resting heart rate and recovery rate as a guide to fitness levels. In circuit training, the number of press-ups or dips achieved in, for example, 30 seconds could also be recorded.

What else will help?

A number of other things could help you reach your goals. For example, you might choose to include a relevant diet; if you are working on building muscle you could decide to include more protein, or if you are doing a lot of long distance activity your intake of carbohydrates might increase, especially before taking part.

Tactics or strategies could also be worked on. The swimmer might change tactics for the next race, not swimming quite so fast on the first length and trying to save some strength for the last one, thereby distributing the pace more evenly over the four lengths.

You must remember that the personal exercise programme is an analysis of the facts and is geared specifically towards improving fitness. The swimming coach might also have observed some technical problems in the swimmer's technique, which could be improved to help to produce a better performance. So the two methods – personal exercise programme and analysis of performance – can work together.

When your personal exercise programme is complete

- Re-test yourself to see how your programme has worked for you.

- Evaluate your programme. Was it successful? How do you know? What could you do (e.g. use progressive overload) to develop it further?

- Write it up. You may wish to present your personal exercise programme as a word document with a title page with your name, exam number (and perhaps your photograph), and a bibliography. These extras will not affect your mark which will be based on the quality of what you have planned, performed, monitored, and evaluated, but doing this will give you an excellent document with a lot of applied knowledge that will be an excellent resource for you to use for your revision and for future reference if you carry on training.

Welcome to ExamZone! Revising for your exams can sometimes be a scary prospect. In this section of the book we'll take you through the best way of revising for your exams, step-by-step, to ensure you get the best results that you can achieve.

> "I felt nervous before my practical exam, but this seems to help me do my best. But I'm not good at written exams and when I looked at the paper, I just panicked." Sarah, GCSE student

Zone In!

Have you ever had that same feeling in any activity in your life when a challenging task feels easy, and you feel totally absorbed in the task, without worrying about all the other issues in your life? This is a feeling familiar to many athletes and performers, and is one that they strive hard to recreate in order to perform at their very best. It's a feeling of being 'in the zone'. Sarah managed this for her practical exam.

On the other hand, we all know what it feels like when our brains start running away with us in pressurised situations, like Sarah. We end up saying lots of unhelpful things like 'I've always been bad at exams', or 'I know I am going to forget everything I thought I knew when I look at the exam paper'.

The good new is that 'being in the zone' can be achieved by taking some steps in advance of the exam. Here are our top tips on getting 'into the zone':

UNDERSTAND IT
Understand the exam process and what revision you need to do. This will give you confidence but also help you to put things into proportion. These pages are a good place to find some starting pointers for performing well at exams.

DEAL WITH DISTRACTIONS
Think about the issues in your life that may interfere with revision. Write them all down. Then think about how you can deal with each so they don't affect your revision.

DIET AND EXERCISE
Make sure you eat well and exercise! If your body is not in the right state, how can your mind be?

BUILD CONFIDENCE
Use your revision time not just to revise content but to build your confidence for tackling the examination.

FRIENDS AND FAMILY
Make sure that they know when you want to revise and even share your revision plan with them. Learn to control them so you don't get distracted and so you can have more quality time with them when you aren't revising, because you aren't worrying about what you should be doing.

COMPARTMENTALISE
You might not be able to deal with certain issues. For example, you may be worried about an ill friend, or just be afraid of the exam. In this case, you can employ a useful technique of putting all of these things into an imagined box in your mind at the start of your revision (or in the exam) and mentally locking it, then opening it again at the end of your revision session.

The key to success in exams and revision often lies in the right planning. Knowing what you need to do and when you need to do it is your best path to a stress-free experience. Here are some top tips in creating a great personal revision plan:

First of all, know your strengths and weaknesses. Go through each topic making a list of how well you think you know the topic. Use your mock examination results and/ or any further tests that are available to you as a check on your self-assessment. This will help you to plan your personal revision effectively by putting a little more time into your weaker areas.

Next, create your plan!

- Find out your exam dates. Go to www.edexcel.com/iwantto/Pages/dates.aspx to find all final exam dates, and check with your teacher;

- Draw up a calendar, or list of all the dates, from when you can start your revision, through to your exams;

- Chunk your revision in each subject down into smaller sections. This will make it more manageable and less daunting. In PE you could follow the order of topics and sub-divisions within topics in the specification, which is clearly divided up already. Revise one chunk at a time, but ensure you give more time to topics that you have identified weaknesses in.

- Make sure you allow time for assessing progress against your initial self-assessment. Just as with your PEP, measuring progress will allow you to see and celebrate your improvement, and these little victories will build your confidence for the final exam;

- Also make time for considering how topics interrelate. For example a long distance runner has good muscular endurance (topic 1.1.3: HRE) in his leg muscles (topic 1.2.4: The muscular system). You will be tested on this in the exam and can gain valuable marks by showing your ability to do this.

Finally (and this is the fun part, I promise!)

Follow the plan! You can use the Know Zone revision section in the following pages to kick-start your revision and for some great ideas for helping you to revise and remember key points. Good Luck!

MAY

SUNDAY

Be realistic in how much time you can devote to your revision, but also make sure you put in enough time. Give yourself regular breaks or different activities to give your life some variance. Revision need not be a prison sentence!

Chunk your revision in each subject down into smaller sections. This will make it more manageable and less daunting.

13

Review Section 3
Complete three practice

Don't plan to start your revision two nights before the exam. Give yourself plenty of time to get through everything.

Review Section 4
Try the Keyword Quiz
27 again

28

In this section you'll find some useful suggestions about how to structure your revision for each of the main topics. You might want to skim-read this before starting your revision planning, to help you think about the best way to revise the content. Remember, different people learn in different ways – some remember visually and therefore might want to think about using diagrams and other drawings for their revision, whereas others remember better through sound or through writing things out. Some people work best alone, whereas others work best when bouncing ideas off friends on the same course. Try to think about what works best for you by trialling a few methods for the first topic.

Remember that each part of the specification will be tested so revise it all.

Can you remember a handful of numbers?

A useful revision technique that many students have found useful throughout my years of teaching is to use this 'handful of numbers'. Each number relates to one of the major topics in section 1.1: and can be used to remember the most important aspects of each.

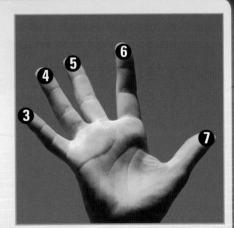

This 'handful of numbers' will help you to recall the key information, because if you can't recall it you can't explain it, and if you can't recall and explain it, you will not be able to apply it, which is what you need to be able to do in the exam.

③ Topic 1.1.1: Physical, mental, social

RECALL: The benefits of taking part are divided into: physical, social and mental.

EXPLAIN: Draw a table with three columns and title them as Physical, Social and Mental. List the benefits that people get from taking part in sport under the appropriate heading. Remember that the benefits of taking part can also be thought of as the reasons why they take part.

APPLY: You need to know the definitions, but also what relevant examples are, so you can apply your knowledge.

Examiner's tip

If you cannot remember the definition exactly, still give an answer and try to define it in your own words as if you were explaining it to your younger brother or sister. Another tip is to go back to it when you are checking your paper near the end of the examination, rather than allowing it to hold up completing the rest of the paper, as something later in the paper may help you remember it more exactly.

❹ Topic 1.1.3: Health, exercise, fitness and performance

RECALL: You should know the definitions for 'Health', 'Exercise', 'Fitness' and 'Performance'.

EXPLAIN: Work with a partner and get them to read out the definitions of these four terms (e.g. health; exercise; fitness and performance), without giving away the actual word. After they have read the first definition you should try to say what word you think it is the definition of. Take it in turns to do this. This is good revision for the multiple-choice questions.

APPLY: Being able to explain how they relate and their contribution to a healthy, active lifestyle is a good way to test yourself on applying this knowledge.

❺ Topic 1.1.3: The 5 aspects of health-related exercise

RECALL: There are 5 aspects of health-related exercise that you need to know.

1. Cardiovascular fitness 2. Muscular strength 3. Muscular endurance 4. Flexibility   5. Body composition.

EXPLAIN: Work with a partner and get them to state a term to be defined; you give the definition. Take it in turns to do this. This is more difficult than the last task but prepares you for this question in the examination. You could also open the task out to include any definition from the glossary.

APPLY: An example of applying one of the aspects of HRE could be: which would be the most important factor for a weight lifter? Muscular strength – go for the obvious answer.

Examiner's tip

Say them in the same sequence each time and then they will flow off your tongue in the examination when you want to remember them.

❻ Topic 1.1.3: The 6 components of Skill-related fitness

RECALL: There are 6 components of skill-related fitness that you need to know.

1. Agility 2. Balance 3. Coordination 4. Power 5. Reaction time 6. Speed.

EXPLAIN: Again, work with a partner and get them to state a term to be defined; you give the definition.

APPLY: In questions you might be asked how a skill is used by a particular sportsperson in their activity, for example: if you are shown a picture of a gymnast on a beam performing a handstand you might be asked to name a skill that the gymnast is using in their performance. Go for the most obvious – balance. Now apply your knowledge and answer the second part of the question; explain how this skill is used in this activity? *"The gymnast needs balance to maintain their position in the handstand and avoid falling off the beam."*

Examiner's tip

Make sure you do not get them mixed up with the health-related exercise terms. Students often make this mistake. If you use a term from the wrong area you cannot get the right answer in any explain or apply questions.

In a multiple choice question you may be asked to give a skill-related fitness term, but in the possible answers there are two health-related exercise terms. If you know which is HRE and which is SRF then you only have to decide between two.

❼ Topic 1.1.4: The 7 Principles of Training

RECALL: There are 7 Principles of Training you need to know.

1. Individual needs/differences 2.Specificity 3.Progressive overload 4.Rest 5.Recovery 6. The FITT principle 7. Reversibility

EXPLAIN AND APPLY: In the exam you could be asked to suggest why a professional marathon runner and a 'fun runner' would have very different training schedules according to their individual needs. Could you answer this?

Examiner's tip

Draw a diagram all of the principles of training on so you can visualise it in the examination room and draw it on a blank page in your examination paper. There will always be a question on this topic so having it to will be very useful.

Other revision areas in Section 1

Topic 1.1.2: Influences and initiatives

You need to know the influences on people taking part in sport, including People, Image etc. You also need to be able to work out what fits with each influence for instance people include: family, peers and role models. You should also know the initiatives (it may even be that some of these are in place in your school and you have experienced them e.g. PESSCL) and understand the different stages of the Sports Participation Pyramid.

Topic 1.1.4: The methods of training

You also need to know and be able to explain the methods of training.

Thinking of them in a table like this might help you to remember them.

Continuous Training	Weight Training
Circuit Training	Interval Training
Cross Training	Fartlek Training

Topic 1.1.5: Your personal health and wellbeing

Before the exam you need to know the factors of a balanced diet, why they are important, and what foods they can be found in:

Macro nutrients – carbohydrate and fats provide most of our energy and protein mainly helps to build and repair muscle.

Micro nutrients – minerals are inorganic substances essential for a healthy body. They include calcium and iron. vitamins are also a micro nutrient.

Water and fibre – water prevents dehydration and fibre is essential for a healthy digestive system.

Revising topics 1.2.1-1.2.5

These topics can be revised in a similar way to those in 1.1 to help you to recall, explain and then to apply your knowledge. Here are some brief notes on each topic.

Topic 1.2.1: Physical activity and your healthy body and mind

RECALL: There are 3 extreme somatotypes types: endomorph, mesomorph, and ectomorph but you should understand that most people are not extreme but a mixture of each type.

EXPLAIN: In applying this knowledge you would need to know and be able to explain that, for example, most top sportspeople are mesomorphs, but in some sports they may have a higher fat tendency, such as some of the bigger rugby players, while a high jumper will be mostly thin but have more muscle than fat.

Examiner's tip

There is a lot to remember in this topic about your body, and the different bodies of other people. All of it is interrelated and you should be able to explain this if required. For example, a mesomorph would be best suited to sprinting because they have a larger muscle girth, giving them more power. As a result of their larger muscle girth they may weigh more than other people their height and be classed overweight.

Topic 1.2.2: A healthy active lifestyle and your cardiovascular system

RECALL: The immediate and short-term effects of exercise on the cardiovascular system.

EXPLAIN: Make sure you can give the definitions of terms relating to the heart. Including heart rate, blood pressure, cardiac output and stroke volume.

APPLY: This could mean being able to say how changes to the heart from regular exercise could improve health, such as a lower resting heart rate could put less stress on the heart.

Examiner's tip

The important thing to know here is what happens to your heart when you start to exercise, and when you have exercised over a period of time: the immediate effects and the effects of regular exercise.

Topic 1.2.3: A healthy active lifestyle and your respiratory system

RECALL: If you are asked to give an immediate effect of exercise on the respiratory system – what is the most obvious? You get out of breath.

EXPLAIN: Two important things to be able to explain are what tidal volume and vital capacity are and that the respiratory system has the important job of providing us with oxygen and getting rid of carbon dioxide in a process called gaseous exchange.

APPLY: When exercising an immediate effect is being out of breath. If exercising at a high intensity athletes cannot get enough oxygen so they experience oxygen debt which will leave them gasping once they finish.

Topic 1.2.4: A healthy active lifestyle and your muscular system

RECALL: Think of what muscles you used and how you used them when you were doing circuit training or weight training exercises.

EXPLAIN AND APPLY: Your knowledge of muscles can be tested in questions in which you need to recall the names of muscles, explain movement and apply your knowledge. Therefore, make sure you know when you are exercising, which muscles are working and what type of movement is taking place.

Examiner's tip

There are 11 muscles that you need to know so break them down into smaller groups and work through them in a logical sequence starting from the top.

Deltoid, then the back: trapezius and latissimus dorsi. Then the front: the pectorals and abdominals. The arms: biceps and triceps. The bottom and legs: the gluteals, the quadriceps, hamstrings and gastocnemius. You must also know how they work: in antagonistic pairs and about the two types of muscle contraction.

Topic 1.2.5: A healthy active lifestyle and your skeletal system

RECALL: You need to know the 3 functions of the skeleton: support, movement and protection.

EXPLAIN: Can you give the definition for all the functions? Ask a partner to test you.

APPLY: You then need to be able to apply it to a sporting situation, and show how each function works. A good example is a gymnast: in a handstand their body is supported and when they perform a forward roll they are able to make their body move – **movement**. Their bones also give them **protection** because if they fell on their head their cranium (skull) would protect their brain. You must also know the joint actions in this section especially around the hinge and ball and socket joints.

Don't Panic Zone

Once you have completed your revision in your plan, you'll be coming closer and closer to The Big Day. Many students find this the most stressful time and tend to go into panic-mode, either working long hours without really giving their brain a chance to absorb information, or giving up and staring blankly at the wall. Some top tips are:

- Plan what you are going to revise beforehand
- Try to revise in silence if possible to get used to examination conditions
- Go over what you have learned until you:
    - know it
    - can recall it
    - can understand it
    - can explain it
    - can apply it
- Chunk the information down into small parts and learn them
    - A chunk might be: health-related exercise
    - Another chunk might be: principles of training
    - Do one chunk per day
- Remember the diagrams and sequences and numbers that fit together – 5 HRE; 6 SRF.
- When you play or watch think how to apply what you have learned for example before a football match the players warm up – why? What are the different parts of the warm up etc?
- Highlight and make a note as you revise any areas that give you particular problems and think of ways to answer these questions.

Last minute learning tips for PE:

Tell your teacher of any problem areas and ask them to give you some past paper questions to do on them; use the text book to help you if you need to. Then get a copy of the mark scheme so that you can see what the examiner was looking for.

Go over the problem areas and answer past paper questions on them, then look at the answers to these questions.

Read your PEP the night before your examination

Exam Zone

Finally, exam day itself will dawn. Here's an overview of what to expect:

On the long course written paper you will have 80 possible marks to be answered in 1½ hours so there should be plenty of time. You'll notice a few different question types on the paper. The examination paper (long course) follows a pattern starting with question 1 which is split into 10 separate multiple choice questions, then short answer questions mostly in the topic order of the specification. The last questions are longer scenarios which may be on any and all parts of the specification. These test your knowledge of the course topics and your ability to apply them to different scenarios. They also test the quality of your written communication so you must write this answer well.

The Short Course paper follows the topic order in the specification but contains mostly multiple choice with a longer answer question at the end of the paper.

Here's an overview of how to do best at each type of question:

Multiple choice questions sometimes ask you to read a number of statements e.g. statements A, B, C, D. You will then be given a choice between whether:

- **A** Both statements are correct, or
- **B** Both are incorrect, or
- **C** The first statement is correct and the second statement incorrect, or
- **D** The first statement is incorrect and the second statement is correct.

In this case as you read through the question it is useful to put a little tick if you think the statement is correct or an x against the statement if you think it is incorrect to help you to follow the question and get the correct answer.

You should always make an attempt at multiple choice questions because you have a 1 in 4 chance of guessing the correct answer. Also, you can sometimes discount one answer because you may be sure that one or even two of the answers are wrong. So, you may now be guessing between two possible answers, not four.

RECALL QUESTIONS

Recall questions are questions that ask you to remember information. You must do well on these questions as they often open up the next part of the question. If you have to go on to describe how to use a principle of training for example in your PEP and you mistakenly use a method of training you will miss out on all the following marks.

EXPLANATION QUESTIONS

Explain means give a reason for something. Explain questions usually have what is called a 'stem' – a little introduction to set the scene. For example:

'Look at the picture of the discus thrower and explain how he uses power in his throw.'

Your answer could be:

'Power is speed times strength (speed x strength) so the discus thrower uses his speed in the turn to get across the circle fast and then uses his strength with this speed at the moment of release.'

APPLYING KNOWLEDGE

You will also be tested on your ability to apply your knowledge in the final question built around a story or scenario. This will be more complex than the short answer questions, but you can learn how to perform well at even these questions.

You can practice your ability to apply your knowledge in many situations even when you are not specifically revising. For example, when you are watching sport on the television listen to the comments from some of the specialists. Listen for the words that they use. For example, a commentator might discuss the "flexibility" of the gymnast, the "reaction time" of the sprinter at the start of the race, and the "cardiovascular fitness" of the marathon runners.

You will also have applied your knowledge when you did your Analysis of Performance and especially in your personal exercise programme. Read your PEP the night before your theory paper examination because if you have planned, performed, monitored and evaluated a good PEP you should know, understand, and be able to explain and to apply it in the theory paper.

GOOD LUCK

Finally, think of this as your cup final. You have completed your practical activities and your Analysis of Performance now visualise that you are ready and better prepared for this examination than any examination you have ever taken before, believe you can do it because you can and you will truly be 'in the zone'.

Good luck, be confident, you can do it!

Zone Out

What happens next? Well, you'll be able to have some well deserved rest time and wait for your results. You'll probably want to start thinking about what you want to do next. If you have enjoyed your PE course there is always the option of carrying on studying and going on to do an A-Level or BTEC course in Sport. For more information on these, go to www.edexcel.com/quals

Glossary for GCSE PE

Aerobic: 'With oxygen'. If exercise is not too fast and is steady, the heart can supply all the oxygen muscles need.

Aesthetic appreciation: To be able to see the beauty in a performance.

Agility: The ability to change the position of the body quickly and to control the movement of the whole body.

Anabolic steroids: Drugs that mimic the male sex hormone testosterone and promote bone and muscle growth.

Anaerobic: 'Without oxygen'. If exercise is done in short, fast bursts, the heart cannot supply blood and oxygen to muscles as fast as the cells use them.

Anorexic: Pertaining to anorexia; a prolonged eating disorder due to loss of appetite.

Balance: The ability to retain the body's centre of mass (gravity) above the base of support with reference to static (stationary), or dynamic (changing), conditions of movement, shape and orientation.

Balanced diet: A diet which contains an optimal ratio of nutrients.

Beta blockers: Drugs that are used to control heart rate and that have a calming and relaxing effect.

Blood pressure: Blood pressure (BP) is the force exerted by the heart as it pumps blood out of the heart and into the arteries (systolic high pressure) and it is low when it relaxes between beats (diastolic).

Body composition: The percentage of body weight which is fat, muscle and bone.

Cardiac output: The amount of blood ejected from the heart in one minute.

Cardiovascular fitness: The ability to exercise the entire body for long periods of time.

Cholesterol: Cholesterol is a blood fat which the body needs in moderate amounts.

Circuit Training: A set of 6 to 10 exercises performed at stations in an organised pattern.
Each exercise is performed for a specified number of repetitions or for a prescribed time before moving on to the next exercise.

Competence: The relationship between: skill, the selection and application of skills, tactics, strategies and compositional ideas; and the readiness of the body and mind to cope with the activity. It requires an understanding of how these combine to produce effective performances in different activities and contexts.

Cooper's run test: A test of cardiovascular fitness.

Coordination: The ability to use two or more body parts together.

Cross training: Using more than one training method.

Diuretics: Drugs that elevate the rate of bodily urine excretion.

Ectomorph: A somatotype, individuals with narrow shoulders and narrow hips, characterised by thinness.

Endomorph: A somatotype, individuals with wide hips and narrow shoulders, characterised by fatness.

Erythropoietin (EPO): A type of peptide hormone that increases the red blood cell count.

Exercise: A form of physical activity done to maintain or improve health and/or physical fitness.

Fartlek training: This type of training allows an athlete to run at varying speeds, over unmeasured distances, on different terrain. (Fartlek is Swedish for 'Speed play')

Fitness: The ability to meet the demands of the environment.

FITT: Frequency, intensity, time, type (used to increase the amount of work the body does, in order to achieve overload).

Flexibility: The range of movement possible at a joint.

Health: A state of complete mental, physical and social wellbeing, and not merely the absence of disease and infirmity.

Health-related exericise: Exercise which is undertaken primarily to improve health and fitness for life.

Healthy, active lifestyle: A lifestyle that contributes positively to physical, mental and social wellbeing, and that includes regular physical activity.

Heart rate: The number of times the heart beats each minute.

Hypokinetic disease: A disease related to too little activity. (Hypo means under or too little: kinetic means energy or activity.)

Hypertrophy: Scientific term for an increase in the size of muscle.

Individual differences/needs: Matching training to the requirements of an individual.

Isometric contractions: Muscle contraction which results in increased tension but the length does not alter, for example, when pressing against a stationary object.

Isotonic contraction: Muscle contraction that results in limb movement.

Joint: A place where two or more bones meet.

Ligaments: A tissue that joins bone to bone.

Mesomorph: A somatotype, individuals with wide shoulders and narrow hips, characterised by muscularity.

Methods of training: Interval training, continuous training, circuit training, weight training, Fartlek training, cross training.

Muscular endurance: The ability to use voluntary muscles many times without getting tired.

Muscle groups: Muscles may be arranged in groups according location and/or function e.g. the muscles of the leg.

Muscular strength: The amount of force a muscle can exert against a resistance.

Narcotic analgesics: Drugs that can be used to reduce the feeling of pain.

Obese: A term used to describe people who are very overfat.

Optimum Weight: Best weight or desirable weight – the best weight a player performs at.

Overfat: A way of saying you have more body fat than you should have.

Overload: Fitness can only be improved through training more than you normally do.

Overweight: Having weight in excess of normal (not harmful unless accompanied by overfatness).

Oxygen debt: The amount of oxygen consumed during recovery above that which would have ordinarily been consumed in the same time at rest (this results in a shortfall in the oxygen available).

PAR-Q: Physical activity readiness questionnaire.

PEP: Personal exercise programme.

Peptide hormones: Drugs that cause the production of other hormones.

Performance: How well a task is completed.

PESSCL: PE and School Sport Club Links.

Physical activity: Any form of exercise or movement; physical activity may be planned and structured or unplanned and unstructured (in PE we are concerned with planned and structured physical activity, such as a fitness class).

Power: The ability to do strength performances quickly (power = strength x speed).

Progressive overload: To gradually increase the amount of overload so that fitness gains occur, but without potential for injury.

Reaction time: The time between the presentation of a stimulus and the onset of a movement.

Recovery: The time required for the repair of damage to the body caused by training or competition.

Rehabilitation: Restoring (an injury) to its normal functioning state.

Rest: The period of time allotted to recovery.

Resistance training: Training that uses a resistance or force against which specific muscle groups must work e.g. weight training.

Reversibility: Any adaptation that takes place as a consequence of training will be reversed when you stop training.

RICE: Rest, ice, compression, elevation (a method of treating injuries).

Role models: A person you can aspire to, to make you into a better person. Often have qualities that we would like to have.

Self-esteem: Respect for, or a favourable opinion of, oneself.

Skill-related fitness: Exercise which may be undertaken primarily to improve sporting ability.

SMART: Specific, measurable, achievable, realistic, time-bound.

Socio-economic status: May be based on a person's income, education, and occupation.

Somatotypes: Classification of body type.

Specificity: Matching training to the requirements of an activity.

Speed: The differential rate at which an individual is able to perform a movement or cover a distance in a period of time.

Stimulants: Drugs that have an effect on the central nervous system, such as increased mental and/or physical alertness.

Stroke volume: The volume of blood pumped out of the heart by each ventricle during one contraction.

Target zone: The range within which an individual needs to work for aerobic training to take place (60–80 per cent of maximum heart rate).

Tendons: A tissue that joins muscles to bone.

Training: A well-planned programme which uses scientific principles to improve performance, skill, game ability and motor and physical fitness.

Training thresholds: The boundaries of the target zone.

Underweight: Weighing less than is normal, healthy or required.

Index (A-F)

Index (P–Z)